Heather Luke's
Creative Curtainmaking
Made Easy

Heather Luke's
Creative
Curtainmaking
Made Easy

Photography by John Freeman

Watson-Guptill Publications / New York

First published in the United States of America in 2001
by Watson-Guptill Publications,
a division of BPI Communications, Inc.,
770 Broadway, New York, NY, 10003

First published in the UK by
New Holland Publishers (UK) Ltd

Library of Congress Cataloging-in-Publication Data
Library of Congress Card number: 00-108784

ISBN 0-8230-1041-4

Designer · Peter Crump
Production · Caroline Hansell
Editor · Judy Spours
Illustrators · Lizzie Sanders, Claire Davies
Editorial direction · Rosemary Wilkinson

2 4 6 8 10 9 7 5 3 1

Reproduction by Pica Colour Separation, Singapore

Contents

Introduction

I hope that the straightforward instructions and detailed step-by-step photographs of the skills and projects in this book will make the process of making curtains easy if you are a complete beginner, and that they will strengthen the techniques of the more experienced maker.

The four main categories of window covering — fold-up shades, unlined sheer curtains, lined lightweight curtains and interlined heavy curtains — are described in detail. Using these skills alone, you can design and create many lovely window treatments. More complicated finishes, such as edgings and borders, embroidery, valances and mixed fabrics can be daunting for the beginner but challenging and exciting for the addicted curtain maker. These are generally covered in less detail, presuming some previous experience. Just tackle those projects that you are confident about; the idea is to enjoy the job and there is neither need nor virtue in making a chore for yourself.

The simplest window treatments can be the most effective and can even be made without a sewing machine or a great deal of working space. Sheer curtains or layers of unlined curtains are very often just hand stitched around with a simple heading and a minimal number of seams — so absolutely anybody can make their own curtains.

Use the ideas and suggestions in this book as a jumping-board for your own creative ideas. Each of the windows illustrated is part of a completed room and does not always show the balance of the whole. Choosing the fabrics for the situation is much more important than how much work you have had to do to make the window covering. The style of your room, its furnishings and the architectural quality of the house will have a great deal of bearing on your choice, as will the view, the relationship with the outside. Use tear sheets from magazines to suggest the latest ideas and trends and period books to confirm and ground your ideas. And remember that simplicity is always the essence of good design.

Select your curtain fabrics both for their color and their texture. For example, fabric of the same color in different textures will look very varied hanging at the window. I often take my inspiration from nature and in particular from food. Nature's colors are rich, luxurious, sensuous and warm. Look at a garlic clove and, depending on the type, you will be able to see colors of ivory, parchment,

Far left An embroidered bed sheet supplied the under curtain, a pair of antique curtains the top layer. Only the striped ticking middle layer has been made for this window. The cross-stripe, bound edges add an extra dimension, but a reluctant maker could stitch a bought trimming to the leading edges and hem instead.

Left Full curtains could easily overpower this little window. Silk and linen in a beach-combing print reflect the scene outside, drawing the eye to the stunning outlook.

Right A handful of stones collected from a beach walk supplied the colors and inspiration for these bathroom curtains.

Far right If you have ever torn open the fruit of a passion fruit plant, you will understand the combination of tangerine and cherry repeated in these hall curtains.

Right Pink-red, rustic matte linen and sensuous shot silk recreate the pitted skin and the juicy bite of a fresh strawberry.

sand, cinnamon, mauve and green. It has textures of tissue paper thinness in the skin, crunchy curly roots and a solid firm sheen as you cut through the bulb. All these can inspire your fabric mixes.

Colors are usually more pleasing in subtle, mid-tones than in complicated or excessive contrast. Textures are pleasing at either end of the scale, from the smoothness of glass to the rough bark of a tree and every way in between. As an example, let's take brown. Your first thought is probably the boring brown and harsh mottled weave of a conference suit or of the decoration in basic hotel chains. Instead, consider the colors of dark cocoa chocolate melting, of flaking shards from cinnamon sticks, of the rolled red skin of a Havana cigar, of the golden brown pitted case of fresh walnut, or of the wet warm black-brown of bog peat. Then there are roasting chestnuts, ground coffee beans, chocolate fudge cake. Brown even smells good. Open a lychee to find the rich red stone inside, shining and already oiled and polished; or dry an avocado stone and watch the many tones as the colors change. Recreate your preferred texture and color with shot taffeta or crunchy linen. If brown can be

this interesting, then so can any other color you care to think about.

Combine plains, plaids, florals, stripes, polka dots, tweeds and any other print or weave in your chosen color field to create both the essence and the complete sense of your chosen style. Above all, enjoy the challenge. Spend as much time as you can in choosing your design, colors and fabrics. Select the best materials you can afford and make window treatments that you feel are achievable. And, if in doubt, keep it simple.

Fabrics

Linen

Linen is arguably the king of fabrics. Harvested from sustainable sources, it is so durable that linen sheets, tablecloths and glass cloths become heirlooms. And the textile can be so fine that it can be used for the most delicate undergarments and nightclothes. Linen fibers are so versatile that anything from the finest, most elegant cloth, to the roughest, rustic fabric can be made on the simplest loom. As a natural fabric, it can help prevent skin irritations.

Linen readily absorbs humidity and is stronger wet than dry. It is therefore ideal as a fabric for under curtains that may come into contact with condensation, and for all other soft furnishings. It looks so good in its plain, woven form that it barely needs a pattern. Herringbone, hop sack and twill weaves are, and have long been, the favored choice for country furnishings. Their nubbly texture seems to fit so well in the uneven and unpredictable countryside.

Linen takes dye only on the surface of the fibers, so as color and decoration wear away, an elegant worn look takes over. Linen is also often woven with silk or cotton to combine the best of their natural properties. More recently, it has been in the vanguard of elegant city decoration, acting as a foil to luxurious silks and soft sensuous velvets.

Linen's only drawback is that it is prone to creasing and involves a lot of work to keep pristine. But it can be washed frequently and at high temperatures, so it is hygienic. Some furnishing linens are now even woven and finished in such a manner that they are almost crease proof.

Left Linen can be finger-pressed accurately, making it a pleasure to work with.

Below Cotton fibers absorb dye best of all the natural fibers. The most intricate patterns and multi-colored designs print 'true'.

Cotton

Cotton has to be the most versatile of all fibers as it takes so many forms — from the finest batiste or organdy to the heaviest velvet damask or bath towelling. The best cotton is harvested from crops grown in the South Sea Islands; the cotton produces the longest and finest filaments. Egyptian, American and Indian crops are of an almost comparable quality. Once the flowers of the cotton plant have died away, soft, hairy fibers can be taken from the downy, white seedpod, called the boll. Twisted and spun to a soft strong thread, these cotton fibers are then woven in many different ways.

Cotton takes dye well and easily, whether it is color of the most delicate pastel tones or the deepest and richest hues. Stronger wet than dry, cotton can be washed inexhaustibly, making it a close second to linen for household furnishings. The finished cloth can be treated in order to make it fire proof, waterproof, stain resistant and in need only of minimum ironing; and it can be plasticized or glazed.

As a curtain material, the self-patterned list of cotton weaves and names is extensive — for example, lawn, organdy, batiste, poplin, canvas, knitted, dobby, herringbone, hop sack, basket, twill, towelling, velvet, damask, pique, matelasse. Adding simple colors to the weaves produces ticking, deckchair stripes and gingham; more complex looms produce damasks, liseres and the most intricate weaves for the fashion and furnishing markets.

Right The light-reflecting quality of silk makes it the most sensuous of fabrics.

Silk

Originating in the Chinese province of Shantung, the production of silk was kept a close secret for many years. Now the most affordable furnishing silks come from Thailand and India, but the yarn has been farmed in both Italy and Prussia and woven most famously in Venice, London and Lyons.

The finest, farmed silk worms are fed on mulberry leaves as the diet produces a whiter thread. The filaments are reeled off while the cocoons are still intact in order to unwind the longest filaments, with few irregularities. The coarser silks, such as tussah, wild silk and matka all come from the larvae of wild moths that lay their eggs in oak trees. The meals of oak leaves produce gray-brown threads and the fine filaments are broken when the moth eats its own way out of the cocoon. These short filaments are joined in spinning resulting in slubs, which even incorporate small pieces of leaf. True silk dupions are made only from twin

cocoons where the silks are reeled off together. Occasional slubs give the irregularities to this characteristic and much copied fabric.

Silk cloth does take dye easily, but the fibers may not absorb the color evenly, which is why there are often shade lines running across the width of the finished fabric. The fiber is strong, absorbent and resilient but is weakest when wet, so careful laundering is required. Silk dye colors are prone to fail if exposed to bright sunlight, especially at south facing windows where the aspect is open. Blue and pink dyes are considered the least stable, so are a little more susceptible to fading than other shades. The newer chemical dyes are designed to stay true and last longer than natural dyes. Potential problems can be forestalled by making a sheer cotton under curtain or shade to hang close against the window.

In order to test silk, hold a piece of the fabric in your hand; real silk will quickly take on your body temperature but imitation silk will stay cold. Two-ply silk can be as smooth and fine as pure gossamer, six-ply strong enough for the toughest upholstery. Curtains can be made from any weight appropriate to the style and design. Always use silk thread when sewing silk fabric, and if it puckers, tack and pin often. Seams can be slightly wetted and finger pressed, rather than heavily ironed.

Wool

The world's primary source of wool is sheep, supplemented by long-haired wool — such as Angora, cashmere and mohair — from goats and rabbits. Wool is a completely natural and sustainable source of textile, as every sheep needs to have its fleece sheared annually, whatever the climate. The inherent properties of the fiber are as you would expect — it is moisture repellant and it supplies warmth by trapping air to retain heat. For a window taking the brunt of the worst weather, wool curtains have to be the best choice.

Both the individual fibers of wool and the woven cloth dye easily and thoroughly, so absolutely any color can be matched or chosen. Wool is often woven together with cotton or silk, both for economy and to make interesting textiles. Wool can be spun into various thicknesses of fiber — the thinnest make the finest, lightest challis and cashmere and the thickest produce dense cut velvet and heavy woven damask. Felted wools can be light and fine or hefty, dense, draft-proofing material.

Wool retains a natural springiness that can make the cloth difficult to handle, but it can be controlled and moulded with the application of steam. Seams also need to be pressed with a hot iron over a damp cloth. Careful laundering is essential. If water is too hot or the fabric roughly handled, the cloth will shrink, or at least felt up, because the fibers, like those of our own hair, are covered with scales. Agitation and heat cause these to open out and tangle up irreparably.

Below **Fine wool worsted for kilts in traditional colors and weaves makes good curtaining fabric.**

Texture and color

Texture and color are the two really important elements of soft furnishings. Subtly varied tones of a single color or gentle contrast of two or three close colors are almost always more pleasing long term than clashing or vibrant contrasts. The most comfortable rooms are often those with only neutral shades or with tones of just two colors.

If you are new to decorating, a simple color board using only natural materials will help you to understand just how subtle the variations of color tone and hue can be to be effective. Collect some or all of the following: a shard of terra cotta pot; a clump of natural or Arran knitting wool; some sand and a few pebbles; a piece of slate, limestone or granite; straw, glass, off-cuts of wood or bark;

Right Inspired use of color and texture in a fabric that complements the landscape beyond.

Colors in harmonious tones exude gentleness and a good feeling in a room.

Most decorating and furnishing mistakes are made from trying too hard and including too many colors and disparate patterns and textures. Consider the integrity of the whole house so that nothing jars or becomes overdone. And choose furnishing fabrics only in colors you feel the most comfortable to be with for a period of time.

Going green

There have been some fantastic revolutions in the development of synthetic fibers in the last few decades, some of which do damage to the environment and some of which do not. As it is usually impossible for the layman and often the professional to tell which is which, it is best to stay as much as possible with one hundred percent natural fibers. Fireproofed fabrics are the exception, as synthetics may be essential: the legal requirement for some purposes and just advisable for others.

Natural fibers usually perform much better than any synthetic copies. Synthetic silk may prove the exception as it now feels and handles exactly like real silk, with all the advantages and none of the drawbacks. It doesn't fade or perish with the sun, it washes in the machine and it doesn't crush. I don't think it has quite the luminosity of real silk, but as an under curtain or to line bed curtains it has no match.

Some interesting developments in new natural fibers might filter through to home furnishings before too long. Abaca – banana leaves – is already being made into rugs, for example, so fine woven fiber suitable for furnishings can't be far away and promises to be most exciting.

a feather and some string; pale rose petals; a cinnamon stick; dried lemon peel; an avocado stone; and anything else you find on the way that can be described as 'natural'.

Another good system for choosing colors and texture is to consider and apply the same principles for furnishings as you do (or would like to do) for your wardrobe. Start with the classics and the basics and look only for good quality. Buy the best you can afford at the time in non-fashion colors. Add 'seasonal changes' or street fashion elements from time to time – when you can afford to and when they are really interesting – to liven up and accessorize the look.

Contemporary fabrics

The newest fabrics are woven with all manner of interesting accessories, such as rubber, string, rose petals, metal filaments or strips of bamboo. These are fabrics for looking at, more sculpture or art than traditional window covering, even to the extent that a single length might be the focal point in a room.

As part of a contemporary setting, flat panels are extremely effective. If they are placed close to a window, daylight plays with the texture and decoration, or they could be used as room dividers, in the manner of Japanese screens. Artificial light might be specially planned and positioned to highlight the nuances of the weave. Whatever the use, keep the making and design simple. The fabric is the star.

Budgeting for fabric

Set your fabric budget at the beginning and allocate it throughout the house. It's no good having one great room and lots of embarrassing ones. Rather, consider the situation and allocate the best fabrics for the major rooms, but use your imagination to make interesting curtains from inexpensive fabrics for secondary rooms. You don't need to spend a fortune on fabrics, but you do need to take the time to look and think before actually making.

Be discerning and don't waste money on wishy-washy pastels or very strong prints in this season's colors. Recently, the 'street fashion' summer colors of bright orange and lime green were translated into large print furnishing fabrics. Fine for a few cushions for one summer, but not to make curtains which you still wish to enjoy in ten years' time.

Don't be tempted either by colors or prints that you will be bored with in just a few months. Think about the wonderful fabrics that have stood the test of time in the wardrobe — felted wools, tweeds, narrow pin or shirt stripes, denim, gingham, calico, velvet and linens.

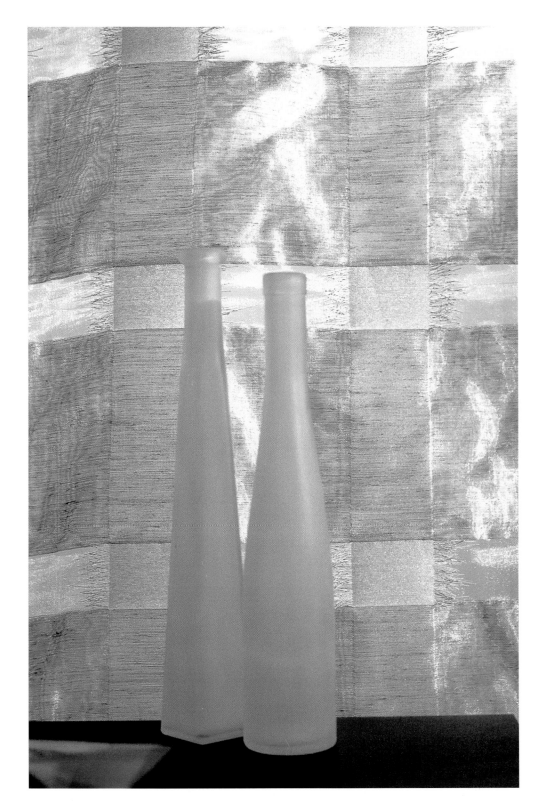

Paper woven into silk organdy is one of the newest fabrics to be used with the other materials currently in vogue: wenge and glass.

Fabrics on a shoestring

I have used bed sheets, duvets, sail cloth, Indian bedcovers, blankets, lampshade silk and even patchworked old clothes as curtain fabrics. The heavy cotton twill decorators' dust sheets, available from any paint merchant, have made the least expensive curtains. They are quite presentable in natural off-white, but just check that they are one hundred percent cotton. They can also be dyed in a bath or washing-machine.

Check out the telephone directory or your local library for information about a textile mill or small factory outlet where fabric lengths can be bought from the sale shop. The most unlikely fabrics can be used to make curtains. I have used lengths of men's suiting, towelling and denim from factory shops when working within a tight budget. Many weavers offer lengths by mail order and some such addresses are given at the back of the book.

Below A few sale remnants costing less than a decent bottle of wine were patchworked in just a few evenings to make what I think are the most charming bedroom curtains.

Mixing patterns

Mixing patterns and fabrics might be reminiscent of gypsy skirts and country patchwork, but it can be great fun and it can work. Christian Lacroix has drawn on the country costumes of Arles for much of his couture design. Ralph Lauren has successfully taken his version of the English look into home furnishings. For

Above and below Traditional fabrics – wool herringbone with printed cotton toile and Scottish plaid with mattress ticking – in interesting combinations for today's homes.

example pinstripes can be mixed with plaids, with floral chintzes, country tweeds, blue denim, blazer stripes and almost anything else.

Perhaps curtains should not be too much of a riot of color or too obvious. The idea is to keep a balance, both of color and scale. Tear sheets from magazines, especially from the fashion pages, and try to make a 'color board' with bits and pieces that you find. Most importantly, the colors should harmonize, not in a boring, humdrum way but in order to complement, contrast and vibrate. As long as you work with fabrics of a similar weight and content, your plan should work.

If you are worried about mixing fabrics together, but love the variety of color and scale, think about mixing color, texture, pattern and print in layers. Again, use magazine pages for your inspiration and to boost your confidence, then track down suitable or possible color swatches and fabric lengths. Hang them together as you perceive the finished result and check how the colors and patterns really work.

There are a number of golden rules about mixing fabrics. Always add at least one and preferably two neutrals to your first color choice. When using one color, mix different textures and tones, which will either vibrate or blend but are seldom wrong. When using two colors, make sure that one of them is clearly in charge. With three colors, balance them carefully in a ratio of 6 to 3 to 1. Pattern on pattern works as long as there is harmony of scale and tone. Checks and stripes work in the same room but can be tricky at the same window. Lastly, don't be afraid to experiment.

Left above and below In these details, glass, jute and wood accessories combine successfully with silk and damask.

Below Plain linen makes a neutral background for luxurious checked silk.

Some successful and exciting combinations of texture, color and weave

silk and wool	spots and flowers	blue and white
linen and organdy	stripes and flowers	sky and corn
leather and linen	very large prints with small prints	cinnamon and russet
velvet and knits	denim with flowers, knits,	taupe and off-white
pin stripes and tweed	tweeds or checks	hyacinth and violet
checks and flowers	tartan and floral	chocolate and almond

Preparation for sewing

Preparation is the key to successful sewing. Prepare well and the work should proceed smoothly, with few errors. Consider various factors before you begin: where you are going to work; what surface you plan to work on; and the fabric you plan to use for the top layer, linings and interlinings. The following are some guidelines to bear in mind before you begin sewing.

The workroom and worktable

A room especially reserved for your use, even if it is only while you are making your curtains, is a real bonus. A dining room or guest bedroom can be made into a temporary workroom with little effort. A worktable at least 2.5 × 1.2 m (8 × 4 ft) and preferably 3 × 1.5 m (10 × 5 ft) is ideal for curtain making. You can buy a sheet of board in either of these sizes, then cover your dining table with thick felt so that the board can be rested safely on top. Alternatively, you could make some sturdy legs which, bracketed onto the underside of the board, make a table that can be fitted temporarily over a guest bed. The space below can be used to store all your fabrics, linings and interlinings and the top will be wide enough for you to work on a whole width of fabric at a time. The height of the worktable should be whatever is comfortable for you; at 1.6 m (5 ft 4 in), I use a table that is 95 cm (38 in) high.

Cover the top of the worktable with heavy interlining and then a layer of lining material. Staple these to the underside, pulling the fabrics very tightly as you go to make a soft surface that is ideal for pinning and pressing.

Cutting out fabrics

First, check fabrics thoroughly for flaws, which are inevitable in a long length. You should have been given some extra fabric to compensate for flaws so that you can organize to cut around them. Try to miss simple line flaws or incorporate them into headings and hems. Holes might be more difficult to work around, so if the fabric is badly flawed in this way, take it back to the seller. When buying fabric, you really do get what you pay for: a market stall bargain is almost bound to be imperfect, while a very expensive designer fabric will rarely come to you with flaws. Those that did occur in weaving or printing will have been cut out before the fabric reaches you.

Measure out each length and mark the cutting point with pins to make sure that you have the correct amount of fabric. Always double-check your measurements before cutting. Fabric should ideally be cut along the grain and to pattern, but sometimes the printing method allows the pattern to move off the grain. Make sure that the leading edges of all pairs of curtains match exactly. If necessary, allow the pattern to run out slightly to either side, although a 2 cm (¾ in) run-off is the most you should tolerate. Do not be tempted to follow the pattern and cut off the grain, as the curtain edges will not then hang straight. As you cut each piece, mark the right sides and the direction of a plain fabric just in case there is a weave variation between the sides which would not otherwise be noticed until the curtains have been made up and hung.

It is best to avoid folding up the lengths of fabric, but if you do need to, make sure it is always lengthwise. We have a series of poles fitted to the wall of the workroom over which each length can be hung until it is ready for use; you might have a banister rail that could serve the same purpose. Join the widths and half widths as planned, using flat seams for all lined and interlined curtains, French seams for lightweight, unlined curtains and flat fell seams for heavy, unlined curtains.

Matching patterns

It is important to make sure that all fabric patterns are matched correctly at the seam on each width. Curtains that are otherwise well made can easily be let down by lack of attention to pattern matching. The following method will ensure that all works well:

1 Place one of the lengths of fabric right side up on the worktop with the selvage facing you. Place the next length over the first, right side down. Fold over the selvage to reveal roughly 0.5 cm (¼ in) of pattern and press lightly.

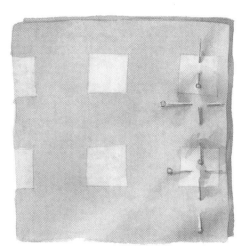

2 Match the pattern to the piece underneath, and pin through the fold line along the whole length. You may need to ease one of the sides at times — using more pins will help. Go back and place cross pins between each pin. Machine or hand stitch along the fold line, removing the straight pins and stitching over the cross pins, leaving them in place.

3 Press the seam from the wrong side and then again from the front. Use a hot iron and press quickly. Turn the fabric over again to the back and press under the seam to remove the pressed ridges. If the background fabric is dark or you are using a woven fabric, snip into the selvages at 5 cm (2 in) intervals. If the background fabric is light, trim the selvages back to 1.5 cm (⅝ in), removing any printed writing.

Bordered fabrics

Some patterned fabrics have printed or woven borders on one or both sides, so before cutting you need to determine where and how to use them. When the border is on both sides of the fabric, decide whether it should appear on the leading and outside edges of the curtain only, or whether one border should appear at each seam — in which case, the extra border should be removed as the widths are joined. I often prefer to remove the center borders and use the extra lengths to allow the border to continue along the hem and, if enough, the heading to 'frame' the curtain.

Where there is a border on one side of the fabric only, it should appear on the leading edge of each curtain. You will need to trim the border off all the way along the length and stitch it back onto each leading edge. Do check whether the border has a directional pattern and if so make sure that you pin it back onto the leading edge accordingly.

Making curtain linings

When you cut out your lining fabric, do so as closely to the grain as possible. Because this is often hard to see, allow about 5 cm (2 in) extra fabric for each cut length. Join the lining widths with flat seams. If your curtains have half widths, it is easier to join all whole widths first and then cut the center width through the middle. This means that you will avoid the annoying possibility of making up two left or right linings rather than a pair. Press all seams so that they lay open.

To make up the hems, place one lining onto the worktable, wrong side facing up, with one selvage exactly along the edge of the table. It is unlikely that the cut line will be exactly straight, so turn up approximately 12 cm (4¾ in) along the lower edge and press in place. Keep this folded line parallel to the bottom of the table. Trim the hem to 10 cm (4 in) from the fold, and then fold it in half to make a 5 cm (2 in) double hem. Pin and machine stitch close to the fold line or slip stitch by hand.

Making curtain interlinings

Interlining should also be cut out to follow the grain. If it is not stitched into the curtain exactly square, after a period of time it will fall down into the hemline. Use the grain line at headings and hems to help you. Join all widths with flat seams and trim them back to 2 cm (¾ in), snipping into the selvage at 5 cm (2 in) intervals.

Curtain weights

For heavy curtains in particular, weights inserted into the hems at each seam and corner will ensure a good hang and drape. Make a lining cover for each weight to prevent it rubbing and possibly discoloring the fabric. Very heavy curtains or sheer curtains should have a length of fabric-covered chain weight threaded into the hem instead. Chain weight is available in different grades to suit various weights of curtain.

Laundering fabric

If your fabric needs to be washed before you work on it, check a small square for shrinkage, particularly if you are making unlined curtains. If your square is smaller after washing than it was before, either wash each length of fabric first or cut longer lengths in order to compensate for future shrinkage.

Planning and measuring

Successful window treatments are those that have been carefully considered and designed before you even purchase the fabric. Unless you are making the most basic pair of curtains, it is helpful to make a scale drawing, particularly when there are windows of different sizes or designs in the same room. You will then be able to experiment on paper with ideas for design and fittings, considering the scale and proportion of both the windows and the room.

Once you have taken accurate window measurements as described below, round them up or down to the nearest 0.5 cm (¼ in) and transfer them to graph paper. If you have neither scale rulers nor graph paper, work with a very simple scale, say, 1 cm = 10 cm or 1 in = 10 in, and an ordinary ruler. Mark the room height, the position of the window and the space around the window. If there is a bay, beam or other obstacle, be sure to mark this in place as well. Don't worry if you have no previous drawing experience, as the examples here are simple to execute.

Secure a piece of tracing paper over your drawn window plan with paperclips, and experiment by drawing onto it different curtains and fitting positions. For example, various tracings could feature long or short curtains, with or without valances or formal or gathered headings. You will soon begin to formulate suitable ideas for the window you are planning.

Once you have a fairly definite concept, draw the window again, tidying up the measurements and draw on the chosen design as accurately as you can. Try to mark exactly where the fittings should be — how far to the side of the window and how far above. If you want

to make a valance, mark the top, sides and center and shape the edge roughly.

Translate your ideas to the window by marking the walls around with a soft pencil and then stand back to look. You will need to make an accurate template for a valance. Most fittings can be cut to size, so ask someone to hold them in place for you to see what they will look like when fixed before you decide on any cuts or changes.

Accurate measurement

Measure the width and height of the window at least three times to make sure that you have accounted for floor or ceiling slopes and whether or not the window is 'square'.

Take the following measurements:

- From the top of the frame or jamb to the floor
- From the ceiling (or under the cornice) to the top of the window
- From the ceiling to the floor
- The window width inside, noting any obstacles, such as telephone sockets
- The window width outside
- The distance available all around the window for the curtain stack-back, clear of bookcases, pictures and so on

Stand back and check for any ugly fittings, such as unsightly double-glazing or unappealing wooden window bars, that may need to be covered. Decide whether you need shades and/or valances or simply fixed curtain headings and plan how and exactly where they should be positioned. If a valance is to be used, make a template and tape it into position to check how it will look.

For curtains to hang outside jamb

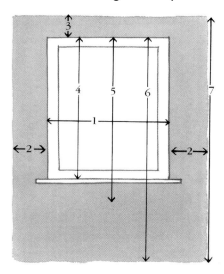

The following measurements are required:

1 Width of window
2 Width of stack-back
3 Top of architrave to ceiling
4 Top of architrave to sill
5 Top of architrave to below sill
6 Top of architrave to floor
7 Ceiling to floor

For curtains to hang inside jamb

The following measurements are required:

1 Width inside frame
2 Length from top of window to sill
3 Depth of frame

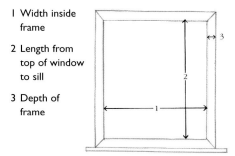

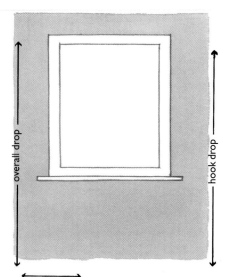

Estimating for curtains

Estimating for curtains

Heading requirements

Heading Type	Fullness Required
Gathered Headings	
Tape	1.75 – 2.25
Ties	1.25 – 2.50
Hand sewn	2.50 – 3.00
Bunched	2.25 – 2.50
Smoked	2.50 – 3.50
Pencil Pleated	2.50 – 2.75
Hand Pleated	
Triple (French)	2.25 – 2.75
Goblets	2.25 – 2.50
Folded	
Pocket	2.00 – 3.00
Voiles	2.50 – 3.00

Most curtains look best with at least double fullness, but this may be reduced for short curtains that do not need the weight to hang well. If the stack-back space is restricted, pleated headings will hold the curtain back into the smallest space. Allow only 1¼ to 1½ times fullness for a heavy fabric or one with a dominant design that needs to be seen.

Heading Allowances

Bunched

Allow enough for a 10–12 cm (4–4¾ in) 'bunch', depending on the thickness of the fabric. Allow the hook drop plus 25–50 cm (10–20 in).

Frilled

Allow the frill above the hook drop and back to fit under the tape. Allow the hook drop plus 12 cm (4¾ in) for a 6 cm (2¼ in) frill, 16 cm (6¼ in) for an 8 cm (3¼ in) frill, etc.

Pencil pleated

Allow the depth of the pleats. Allow the overall drop plus 6–8 cm (2¼–3¼ in).

Pocket headings

For voiles, allow 2 cm (¾ in) for the pocket and 2 cm (¾ in) above. Allow the overall drop plus 8 cm (3¼ in).

Bound headings

No allowance needed. Overall drop, no extra.

Smocked

Allow the depth of the smocking pattern. Allow the overall drop plus the depth of the smocking pattern.

Goblet/triple pleats

Allow double the depth of the pleat. Allow the overall drop plus 20 cm (8 in) for a 10 cm (4 in) pleat. Allow the overall drop plus 30 cm (12 in) for a 15 cm (6 in) pleat.

Hem allowances

Unlined curtains	16 cm (6¼ in)
Lined curtains	16 cm (6¼ in)
Lined, bound hems, plain lining	8 cm (3¼ in)
Lined, bound hems, contrast lining	No extra fabric
Interlined curtains	12 cm (4¾ in)
Voile curtains	8–12 cm (3¼–4¾ in)

Estimating for curtain fabric

The amount of fabric you need for each window is relative to the style of curtaining that you wish to make. The three factors to bear in mind are: the headings style; the fullness; and the curtain length. You will have already chosen your window treatment following the guidelines on page 18 and from this you will know the fittings width and overall drop of the curtains.

The hook drop is the measurement from the top of the curtain hook and the bottom of the curtain fitting to the hemline. The overall drop is from the top of the heading to the hemline. Before the fittings are in position, you will need to estimate these measurements from your plan.

Make allowances for any proposed alterations to the room — for instance, cupboards to be fitted close to the window or a change of flooring.

Curtain lengths

Use the following as a guide for calculating the amount of fabric you need for each curtain length.

1 Find the overall drop.

Ceiling to floorboards	270 cm (106 in)
Less allowance for carpet of 2 cm (¾ in)	268 cm (105¼ in)
Less allowance for valance board of 2 cm (¾ in)	266 cm (104½ in)
Plus overlong hem allowance of 5 cm (2 in)	271 cm (106½ in)

2 Add the hem and heading allowances.

Hem	12 cm (4¾ in)
Heading	20 cm (8 in)
Each cut length	303 cm (119 in)

3 Adjust for pattern repeat, if necessary.
If the pattern repeat is 65 cm (25½ in)

303 cm + 65 cm = 4.66

(119 in + 25½ in = 4.66)

Round up to 5.

Allow 5 repeats for each cut, as each cut length must include complete pattern repeats.

5 x 65 cm = 325 cm

(5 x 25 in = 127½ in)

Each cut length will need to be 325 cm (127½ in).

Note that the fabric 'wastage' of 325 cm (127½ in) is needed for each cut, yet only 303 cm (119 in) is actually needed for the curtain — so five pieces of 22 cm (8¾ in) will be left. You can decide how best to use this spare fabric, perhaps to alter headings — for example, to have a frilled and bound heading rather than a bound only — or to increase the heading fullness from frilled to bunched.

Or this spare material could be allocated for tiebacks, valances and the like, depending on the amount of fabric available. Fabric valances can otherwise be very expensive, and the advantage here is that the pattern is already matched.

Planning the fabric in this way means that you will never have wasted pieces, and you will be aware when cutting of the importance of using fabric wisely. If the fabric you have chosen is expensive and the estimated cuts are just over a whole repeat (that is, 4.1 repeats), you could shorten the hem or heading

allowance a little without damaging the hanging quality.

Always allow an extra pattern repeat to the total amount of fabric estimated to allow you to start your hemline in the position on the pattern that you choose.

Curtain widths

Use the following guidelines to estimate the number of curtain widths you will need.

1 Select your fitting and divide the length in half for two curtains.

180 cm ÷ 2 = 90 cm

(70 in ÷ 2 = 35 in)

2 Add the side return (10 cm/4 in) and the center overlap (10 cm/4 in)

90 cm + 10 cm + 10 cm = 110 cm

(35 in + 4 in + 4 in = 43 in)

3 Multiply by the fullness needed for your heading.

110 cm x 2.5 = 275 cm

(43 in x 2.5 = 107½ in, say 108 in)

4 Divide by the width of your fabric.

275 cm ÷ 135 cm = 2.04

(108 in ÷ 54 in = 2)

Therefore, use two cuts per curtain.

5 Multiply the number of widths by the cut lengths.

For plain fabric:

303 cm x 4 =12.12 meters

(119 in x 4 = 13¼ yards)

You will need 12.12 meters (13¼ yards)

For patterned fabric:

325 cm x 4 = 13 meters

+ 65 cm for extra repeat = 13.65 meters

(127½ in x 4 =14 yards

+ 25½ in = 14¾ yards)

You will need 13.65 meters (14¾ yards)

Making templates

Make accurate templates of any features of the room that might prevent curtain drapes from hanging well. Cornices will usually be above the curtaining, but sometimes the side of the valance will need to return onto the cornice. Otherwise, a plate rack, picture rail or pipes might obstruct the fall of the curtains.

Ideally, use brown paper and a pencil to draw around any obstacle. If this is not possible, tear the paper roughly and cut in around it accurately with a sharp knife.

Hand-pleated headings

Aim to make pleats of 15 cm (6 in) with gaps between pleats of 12 cm (4½ in). For a fitting size of 195 cm (76½ in), each curtain will be:

97.5 cm + 10 cm + 10 cm = 117.5 cm

(38¼ in + 4 in + 4 in = 46¼ in).

Use the following guidelines to estimate how to accommodate pleats.

1 Work out the number of pleats and gaps.

97.5 cm ÷ 12 cm = 8.13

(38¼ in ÷ 4½ in = 8½)

2 Work out the fabric needed for the pleats.

9 x 15 cm = 135 cm

(9 x 6 in = 54 in)

Preparations for shades

3 Add this plus side turnings to the curtain width.

117.5 cm + 135 cm + 12 cm = 264.5 cm

(46¼ in +54 in + 4½ in = 104¼ in)

4 Divide this by the fabric width.

265 cm ÷ 135cm = 1.96

(104¼ in ÷ 54 in = 1.92)

Round this figure up to allow two widths of fabric for each curtain.

If this calculation had worked out so that there was spare fabric in the widths, you could increase the size of the pleats to accommodate it or cut away the excess. Conversely, if the fabric requirement calculated that you would only just need to cut into a full width, you could use slightly less fabric in each pleat.

If your room has two or more windows of various widths, all the curtains should have exactly the same size pleats and distance between pleats. In this case the widths will need to be cut down to exact measurements for each curtain.

Fittings for shades

Most fabric shades are fixed to wooden battens to hold the fittings necessary to operate them. The headings, whether flat, pleated or gathered, must be made up to fit the batten size. Touch and close tape is usually used to hold the shade to the batten, with one piece stapled or tacked to the batten and the other stitched to the back of the shade heading. Small colored tacks may also be used to fit the shade to the batten.

Roller shades have a roller and fixing brackets included in the kit. Make sure that you follow the manufacturer's instructions when assembling the shade.

Rolled-up shades will fit to a batten as above, but instead rely on attached tapes, cords or ribbons to raise and lower them to the position required.

Cascade, Roman, London, Austrian and festoon shades all depend on the pulley system of a series of cords threaded through rings at regular intervals across the shade to operate them.

Each shade design will require different spacings between the cords, and these will be planned with the overall design. The instructions for making up generally show where and how the rings on the shades should be fitted and how the cords need to be fixed and threaded through the rows of rings.

Making a batten

Cut a piece of wood 5 x 2 cm (2 x ¾ in) to the finished width of the shade. Cut a length of fabric 4 cm (1½ in) longer than this and 15 cm (6 in) wider. Apply glue to the back of the batten (one of the 5 cm/2 in sides) and wrap the fabric tightly

around. Staple or tack one side of some touch and close tape to the top at the front of the batten. Stitch the other piece of touch and close tape to the shade heading. The batten is now ready to be fitted to the shade.

Mark the batten in line with the row of rings and the cords. Take the shade away and fit either brass screw eyes or china thimbles at these points, to carry the cords. You must now decide from which side you prefer to operate the shade. Fit the batten in position on the window and fit the cleat that will hold the cords in a convenient position.

Thread the cords through, starting with the side away from the operating fittings. Thread the first cord through all the rings to the opposite side of the shade, the second cord through the next ring and so on. When you have threaded through all the cords, hold them together and pull the shade up as high as possible. Adjust the pleats, raise and lower the shade at least two or three times to ensure that the cords are free and the shade hangs straight.

With the shade lowered, knot the cords together at the bottom of the cleat. Raise the shade, secure the cords and adjust the pleats, folds or gathers. Check now that the shade is still hanging straight and if it is not, retie the cords. Thread the cords into a cord weight, knot and trim away the excess.

Shades can also be fitted to poles, but the same batten will need to be fitted just behind the pole so that the shade can be raised and lowered efficiently.

The size of the batten should be altered to suit your situation. Shades may be fitted flat against the frame, or forwards to avoid window fittings. Fit into the ceiling, the window frame or with small brackets.

possible positions of battens

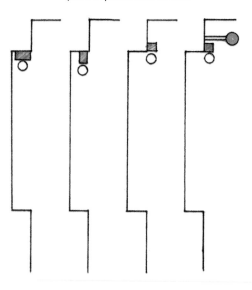

Measuring for shades

Once you have chosen the design of the shade and the position of the fittings, take accurate measurements in order to find the finished width and the overall drop. Final measurements can only be taken once the fittings are in place, but an estimate will enable you to order the correct amount of fabric required.

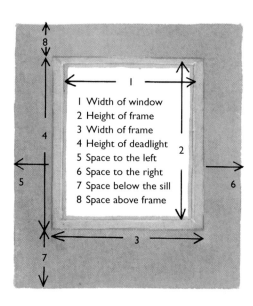

1 Width of window
2 Height of frame
3 Width of frame
4 Height of deadlight
5 Space to the left
6 Space to the right
7 Space below the sill
8 Space above frame

As all shades need to be raised and lowered without interruption, they need to be made exactly 'square'. Very few windows have four corners absolute at right angles, so use a set square or leveler to determine the top line. Lightly pencil the top line on the frame or wall from which the measurements will be taken and to which the batten will be fitted. Measure both the width and the drop at 20 cm (8 in) intervals. The narrowest or shortest measurement is the one which you must use to be sure that the shade can be raised and lowered without trouble.

Special care needs to be taken with cottage or very old windows, where walls and plastering are uneven, as the shade space may vary considerably. Most shades can be made to fit windows with shaped tops, such as arches, although round windows are more difficult. The easiest arched tops to work with are those with a fairly shallow curve. The shade will only pull up to the bottom of the curve, so consider the amount of available light that might be blocked. You will need to mark a horizontal line as near to the bottom of the arched shape

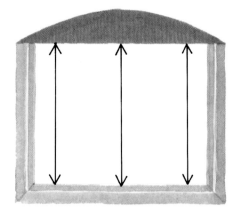

as possible. Cut a paper template of this arch, using the line you've just drawn as the bottom of the template. Measure from this line to the sill, or to the bottom of the shade.

If you want to make cascade, Austrian or festoon shades, you will need to know how full they will be. Use a strip of fabric, piece of string or length of lightweight chain and tape this to the window to see the sort of hem shape you can make. When you are happy, remove the tape and measure the total length and the length of each swag. This will represent the finished width of the shade.

Estimating fabric

Regardless of the size of your window, each different style of shade will require a different quantity of fabric. A rolled-up shade, for example, will need much more than a flat Roman shade. The cost of the fabric may determine your choice of shade, although the style of room and furnishings will be your first guide.

The following example demonstrates how to estimate the amount of fabric you will require for Roman shades.

Decide whether the shade is to fit inside the window jamb, against the frame or outside the jamb, to the wall or an outer frame. To the finished width and the overall drop, add 12 cm (4¾ in) for the side turnings and 6 cm (2¼ in) for the hem, plus heading allowance of 2–3 cm (¾–1¼ in).

For a finished width of 150 cm (60 in) and overall drop of 200 cm (79 in), each cut length will be:

200 cm + 3 cm + 6 cm = 209 cm

(79 in + 1¼ in + 2¼ in = 82½ in).

The number of widths needed will depend on the width of your fabric, say 130 cm (51 in).

150 cm + 12 cm = 162 cm

÷ 130 cm = 1.24

(60 in + 4¾ in = 64¾

÷ 51 in = 1.25), say 2.

2 × 209 cm = 418 cm

(2 × 82½ in = 165 in or 4½ yd).

The number of folds in the shade will affect the amount of space it occupies when pulled up. As a general rule of thumb, aim to make a shade that will take up approximately 17–19 cm (7–7½ in) of space when folded up. Bear in mind that you will be stitching a rod at the top of each fold. The distance between the rods will be 30–34 cm (12–13½ in). The lowest section should be 1–2 cm (⅜–¾ in) more than half the distance between each rod.

Take the finished drop of the shade and deduct 2 cm (¾ in). Divide the rest by approximately 15 cm (6 in). You will need an uneven number, so try dividing by amounts between 15–17 cm (6–7 in) until you have a satisfactory figure. For example, for a finished length of 116 cm (45½ in):

116 cm - 2 cm = 114 cm

(45½ in - ¾ in = 44¾ in)

114 cm ÷ 15 cm = 7.60 cm

(44¾ in ÷ 6 in = 7½ in)

Using 7 as the nearest uneven number,

114 cm ÷ 7 cm = 16.29 cm

(44¾ in ÷ 7 in = 6½ in). The folds of the shade will be 16.29 cm + 2 cm (6½ in + ¾ in) for the lower section and 32.58 cm (12½ in) for each of the other sections. Round these figures up to 18.3 cm and 32.6 cm (7 in and 13 in).

This example requires three folds and therefore three rods. (The lining cuts will need to include 6 cm (2¼ in) extra for each rod pocket.)

Making linings for shades

Buy good quality lining fabric as it will wear well. This is particularly important for shades, which are often raised and lowered at least twice a day.

Cut out your lining fabric as close to the grain as possible. Because this is often hard to see, allow approximately 5 cm (2 in) extra for each piece. Join all lining widths with flat seams.

Buy lining the same width as your main fabric if possible; otherwise, cut down a wider lining fabric to match the top fabric width before joining.

Unstructured shades

Wherever possible, the lining seams must match the fabric seams. Apart from helping to keep the fabrics straight, all seams show up against the light when the shades are in position, so the making methods must be as neat and unobtrusive as possible.

Press all seams flat both front and back to remove any ridges, fold linings lengthwise and rest over a long table or banister rail to keep everything straight.

Rodded shades

Cut the lining lengths to the length of the finished shade, adding an extra 6 cm (2¼ in) for each rod pocket. Join the widths to match the overall width of the main fabric, and trim to exactly the finished shade width. Place the lining onto the worktable with the right side facing down. Press over 3 cm (1¼ in) along each long side.

Starting from the bottom, and using a set square, trim the hemline of the lining material exactly square with the two sides. Measure from this line up to mark the position of the lowest rod pocket, in two rows 5 cm (2 in) apart. Use a set square to make sure that you keep these lines exactly at right angles to the sides of the shade.

Measure from this line to the next, then 6 cm (2¼ in) and repeat to the top. Check that the distance between the top of the shade and the top of the top rod pocket is correct.

Draw a light pencil line at the top and bottom of each rod pocket to mark its position. Fold together and stitch one each in turn. Press the rod pockets upwards and leave on one side.

Interlining shades

Cut the interlining to the same size as the linings, as it will be trimmed to correspond to the exact size of the finished shade during the making. Use only sarille interlining or a light to medium weight cotton bump. Interlining gives a good, soft finish but for shades should not be too obviously thick and padded. Join all widths with flat seams and trim back to 1.5 cm (⅝ in).

Curtain fittings

Curtain tracks

For most uses, metal tracks with plastic runners and an enclosed pull-cording system are the best. These are available in several different qualities to suit the weight and length of your curtains and are easily adaptable to 'top fit' onto a valance board or into the recess, or to 'face fit' to the wall or directly onto the window frame. They are available in telescopic lengths to suit a wide range of window sizes or can be cut to size. You can also buy small tracks specifically for sheer curtains that often need to be fitted invisibly behind a pole or into a space behind the main curtains.

Side fittings, which hold the track to the wall, come in several different sizes, so that the track can be fitted either very close to the wall or a distance out. This allows the curtains to hang straight if over a radiator or deep sill.

Cording

Is essential to protect interlined and long curtains, particularly if they are of lightly colored fabric. Even the natural oil of the hand will cause a buildup of grime on the curtain edge in time. Cords to close the curtains will prevent any such damage. Any window that is taller than it is wide can work with cords and weights heavy enough to keep the cords taut. Also fit 'S'-clips to prevent the cords twisting.

You may prefer to fit a pulley system that will keep the cords running in a continuous loop. This method is essential where the windows are wider than they are high. It is especially useful for a bay window with short curtains, as the pulley can be fixed to the edge of the sill, behind the curtains and out of sight.

Track covers

Tracks are best unseen, so make a track cover to disguise the fittings. Cover it in the same fabric as the curtains or paint it to blend in with the wall. Make the top with wood and the front with plywood. The brackets will then need to be housed into the wood to allow the fabric cover to fit neatly.

Cover the top, front and inside of the board with interlining and then the whole item with fabric. Starting at the back, work across the top, down the

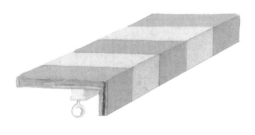

front and inside. Glue only in three places — at the back on the topside and underside, and inside where the 0.5 cm (¼ in) front joins the board. Fit it onto the wall and camouflage the center bracket and any side brackets with wallpaper or paint.

Valance boards

Valance boards need to suit the quality and weight of the curtaining and valances. Always add sides and fronts to the valance board to keep the valances from brushing against the curtains and to prevent the valance tipping backwards. Use wood for the top and 0.5 cm (¼ in) plywood for the front, with substantial brackets to hold the weight.

Paint the board to match the window frame or cover the whole board with

fabric to match the curtains. Ensure that the track is fitted approximately 5 cm (2 in) from the front of the board so that the heading can draw freely, but without leaving a large gap. For a shaped board, choose a track that will bend to follow the front line.

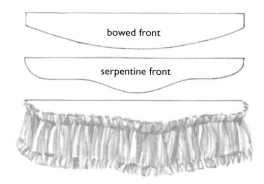

bowed front

serpentine front

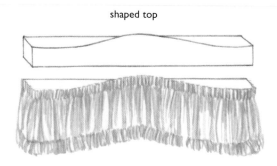

shaped top

Curtain poles

There are so many different types of pole and finial style available that you will be spoiled for choice. Choose poles that can be fitted as closely to the wall as possible, with brackets that have fixings above and below the pole, otherwise heavy curtains could pull the fitting away from the wall. The end brackets should be positioned so that there is approximately 3 cm (1¼ in) from the fitting to the end of the pole, just enough space for one curtain ring. The curtain will then pull right to the end of the pole.

From the plainest black metal, supplied by a blacksmith, to the most elaborately carved and gilded, the choice of pole is as essential to the overall design as the color, weight and fullness of the curtains. Fashions change and availability with them, but at the moment metal poles are in vogue. They are good for cottage windows or wherever space is limited and the fitting needs to be insignificant. Any rustic window or country-style room will benefit from narrow poles and interesting finials. They are always available in black, but can be overpainted with cellulose or stencil paints and a water-based varnish to prevent the smell of cellulose or if you prefer using a brush to dealing with spray paint.

Wooden poles from 2.5 cm (1 in) in diameter to 10 cm (4 in) in diameter are the other most frequently used option. Narrow poles are fine for a small window with curtains sitting inside, and most rooms work best with poles of 5–7 cm (2–3 in) in diameter. If you have a lot of height in the windows and space around them, you need seriously chunky fittings: any size can be made to order from a good craftsman, but antique markets can be a good source.

Poles sleeved in hand-stitched leather are a luxurious — but expensive — option for the right room. Glass and acrylic poles look fantastic with lightweight curtains. If you really want to push the boat out, combine glass poles with the best silk taffeta for a light, contemporary look. If you love glass poles but have a limited budget, hang antique linen sheets or tea towelling material, which costs very little.

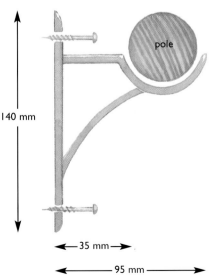

Dressing curtains

Formal styles

Hand-headed curtains need to be dressed as soon as they are hung so that the pleats are trained to fall evenly. You will need to leave the curtains tied back for at least 48 hours and possibly up to 96 hours. The waiting will be well rewarded, as your curtains will always hang well thereafter.

Begin by drawing the curtains to the stack-back position. Make sure that the heading is in order, the pleats are arranged forwards and the gaps are folded evenly between each pleat. If the curtain hangs under a track or pole, the gaps will fold behind; if in front, the gaps will fold to the front.

Stand at eye level with the headings and take each pleat, smoothing it down through the curtain as far as you can reach to form a fold. Now, standing on the floor or lower down the stepladder and starting at the leading edge, follow these pleats through to waist height. From the leading edge, fold each pleat back onto the last. Tie a strip of fabric loosely around the curtain to hold the pleats in place.

Kneel on the floor and follow the folds through into the hem. Finger press them into place firmly.

If the curtains are over long, keep the pleats together and bend the curtain to one side. Tie another strip of fabric around the curtain hem to hold the pleats in place, loosely enough not to mark the fabric but tight enough that they do not slip down. Springy fabrics may need to be readjusted several times, but this will become easier as the pleats are trained.

Informal styles

If you want your new curtains to fall into soft folds, or to look as though they have been there for a long time, try one of the following window dressing ideas. Either pull the curtains back and forth about a hundred times to unstiffen the fabric, or pick them up, pull them towards you and drop them down again, until they have settled in nicely.

Formal pleated headings are only chosen when you want the curtains to hang in a controlled, even manner. Dressing the pleats soon after hanging trains the fabric to pleat back in folds.

Informal headings are suitable for informal curtains, where a freer, easier, less studied finish is required. The curtain tiebacks can also be comparatively casual in style.

Curtain care

Regular care and attention will prevent curtains becoming dirty. If disaster strikes, if someone in your household smokes or you light open fires, or if you are moving house and want to make alterations, use a specialist cleaner. Do choose one used to handling handmade curtains and, if possible, one who will come and clean them on site.

Washing

Unlined curtains are often made for situations where regular cleaning is necessary, according to the fabric manufacturer's reccomendations. If frequent washing is essential, use a strong, hardwearing fabric, such as cotton, with enough substance to stand regular handling.

Firstly, check the washing label attached to the roll of fabric. Then test a small off-cut of the same fabric. Cut an exact square or rectangle and write down its measurement — 10 x 15 cm (4 x 6 in) is usually enough. Check the size again after pressing the washed sample. If there is shrinkage and you haven't allowed for it when making the curtains, then either wash at a very low temperature, or dry clean.

Make sure that every trace of detergent is removed. Sunlight can react with the residue of cleaning chemicals and cause fading. Always press when still damp, as pressing and steaming will keep the fabric in shape. Try not to press over seams; only press up to them with the point of the iron. If you do need to press over a seam, slip a piece of cloth between the seam and the main fabric to prevent a ridge forming.

Dry cleaning

This is the only realistic option for interlined curtains, or for any curtains where more than one texture has been used. But generally, unless accident or smoke makes cleaning inevitable, dry cleaning should be avoided in favor of regular vacuuming and airing.

Airing

The best and most effective way to keep curtains clean and fresh is to choose a slightly breezy day, open the windows wide, close the curtains and allow them to blow in the breeze for a few hours. This will remove the slightly musty lining smell. If you can do this every few weeks, your curtains will always stay fresh. This is more of a problem in the city, but is possible if you choose quiet, breezy, sunny spring and autumn days.

Vacuuming

The regular removal of dust is vital to prevent particles of household dust settling into the fabric grain, as once dirt has penetrated, it is very difficult and often impossible to remove satisfactorily. Vacuum all soft furnishings regularly with a soft brush, paying special attention to the inside of chair seats, pleats and frills. For delicate fabrics and valances, make a muslin or fine calico 'mob cap', elasticated to fit over the end of the brush, to soften the bristles and minimize fabric abrasion.

Alterations

If curtains need to be altered for any reason (such as moving), have them cleaned by a specialist dry cleaner before alterations are carried out. Remove stitching from the sides and hems to allow any ruckled fabric to be cleaned and to allow the fabrics to shrink to different degrees.

Track maintenance

Periodically spray the inside of the curtain track and the top of poles with an anti-static household cleaner or silicone spray to prevent dust building up and to ease its running. Poles may be cleaned with a diluted household cleaner and a soft brush to remove dust from the crevices of decorative finials and the underside of curtain pole rings.

Fire-proofing

Some fabrics are required by law to be fire-retardant, either as part of the weave or by a subsequent treatment of the fabric. If you are making curtains for a hotel, sports club, holiday accommodation or for any commercial building, you must check the current regulations and your supplier to make sure that the fabric you have chosen will pass the relevant tests. Many fabric companies produce special ranges that comply. If you need advice, there are a couple of contacts listed at the back of the book.

Tiebacks

The practical purpose of tiebacks is to keep curtains fixed back out of the way. For example, they are useful at door openings and to the sides of windows, where space is severely restricted. They also keep curtains out of harm's reach — in the form of children, pets, water and visitors, to name the most obvious. Tiebacks don't need to be made much of if they're not supposed to be show stoppers. A simple loop of cord, a tie or twisted fabric are economical and effective. Show stoppers, on the other hand, are primarily decorative, although they may have a practical function as well — for instance, to allow light into a room. But the drape of the curtain and the tieback itself are the main players.

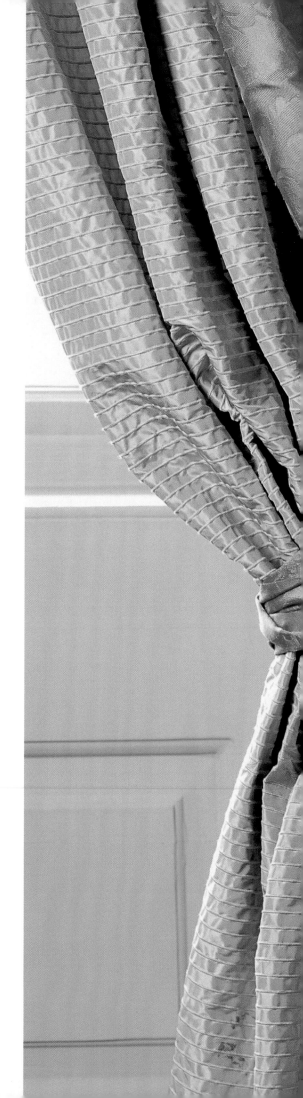

Positioning a tieback

The position of a curtain tieback is crucial. The curtain above the tieback needs to be given enough space to make a good drape, especially if a fringe is to be shown off, but the hem also needs space to fan out beneath. Try holding the curtain back with approximately two thirds of the material above, one third below. Work up or down a little from this point to get the best position for your window. Alternatively, you can deliberately choose to fit the tieback high up, especially at a bay window, or at a small window where daylight is at a premium. Drape the curtain so that the fabric above the tieback is not too tight and so that the curtain beneath hangs beautifully, twisting to show an attractive lining, perhaps.

Above left Cord loops in colors to tone with the curtain fabric hold the curtain back neatly, without undue fuss or drama. Choose like for like — cords woven in linen and/or cotton for linen and cotton fabrics, silky cords for fabrics with sheen and wool with heavy cottons and wools. Tieback hooks need to be long enough that the curtains aren't pinched back too tightly at the side.

Center left Combinations of opposite textures, especially shiny and matte, are interesting to look at and important for a luxurious contemporary look. Here curtains in a silk and jute damask weave are finished with tiebacks in jute and polished wood.

Below left Waxed string threaded through antique bobbins or old reels make great tiebacks.

Above right Curtains hung instead of a door between bedroom and dressing room are rarely drawn. The brass holdbacks are decorative as well as functional, keeping the tasselled tiebacks in place.

Center right Chunky cotton tassels complement the texture and country style of toile de Jouy curtains and provide good contrast to the fine silk of the under curtains.

Below right Silky tassels woven in rich colors complement both the brocade and moiré fabrics of this doorway curtain and the velvet furnishings in the adjoining room.

Choosing a style

Buy tieback fittings that look good with the curtain fitting and with the window furniture. If your bathroom is all chrome or pewter or satin steel, for example, have fittings to match. Painted wood or metal poles need painted fittings to match; brass goes with brass and also looks good with wood. You might need tiebacks colored silver or gold, and stencil paints will be fine brushed over a painted base. Add a layer of clear varnish and then a little dark polish to knock back the tone.

Curtains might need to be tied back more often than they are left to drape down. The tieback then becomes an important feature and you might want to splash out on something rather special. You can have a tieback made to whatever figure you care to put on it. Copies of tiebacks made for the palace of Versailles and other, less extravagant antique finds can cost hundreds.

Above and center left Where just one pair of curtains in a sequence of layers needs to be held back, the best solution is a brass or other metal holdback. With cord or fabric tiebacks you need to take the tieback around the curtain, which can be awkward when there are multi-layers. Metal arms are fitted to the wall or woodwork behind the curtain and the curtain is picked up and hooked into the loop.

Below left If a shade is used regularly and the curtains are not needed very often, you can just pin the fabrics together in whichever position you choose. Here we pinned on a pretty antique brooch, but hair clips, earrings, hat pins or even cufflinks could be used.

Above right Manufactured tiebacks usually only come with one standard cord length. For differently sized windows in the same room, the cord length might need to be adjusted so that the tassels all hang in the same position. It is not possible to cut the cords, so slip the knot forwards to look right from the front and stitch the excess cord into a loop at the back where it won't be seen.

Center right Glass chandelier drops tied together with cords and ribbons sit well with other light-reflecting materials, especially silk taffeta.

Below right If possible, buy the tieback hooks and holdbacks in the same metal as the window catches.

Decorative tiebacks

If I want the curtain to speak for itself, I might make the tieback a sash or long tie from the same fabric, so that the whole curtain has some panache and interest without appearing pretentious. Decoration can be fun in an appropriate setting. Real flower twists can be used to herald a new season, or for a party; silk flowers can provide a dramatic effect, stunning against a contrasting plain fabric. Wooden beads, glass grapes, bangles, chandelier drops, shells, and many other finds can be worked into most effective and individual decoration, whether permanent or for an occasion.

Above left A long tie might be fiddly for a curtain in constant use, but here the curtains are usually kept back, so the tieback is decorative and the double cross efficient.

Above If you want to show off the lining as much as the front of the curtain, a small fabric loop stitched into the curtain is enough to keep the drape in place.

Above right A long tie in the same fabric allows the method to be as inconspicuous as possible, allowing the stitch work and the colors of the curtain to star.

Left A leather jacket button provides interesting detail and complements the Scottish tartan.

Right Double sash bows in sumptuous silk do hold the curtains back but are deliberately decorative, mimicking the idea of the bow on the bustle of an evening gown.

Bell Tiebacks

◀◀ **see also** ▶▶
Silk p. 9   Ties p. 152
Gathering stitches p. 147

These tiebacks have a Renaissance feel about them and I think will always be most effective made with a silk, velvet or other luxury fabric. In any case, you need a textile which will gather easily and reflect light. I don't think it's appropriate to give particular measurements for these tiebacks, as the width and height of your window will determine the proportion and size of the finished bell. If you are in doubt, always scale up rather than down. You will need to stuff each section with something; we usually use very thick cylinder wadding, but interlining, polyester wadding or old stockings will do just as well. You will also need a key tassel for each.

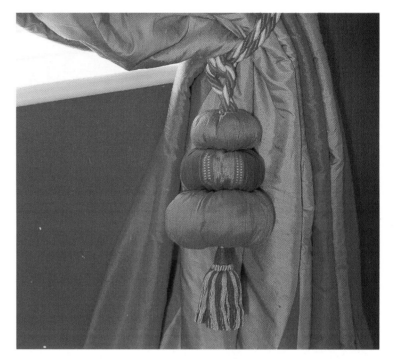

Preparation: Cut a piece of fabric 40 cm × 20 cm (16 × 8 in) and join the two short ends together. Gather the bottom end and stuff until it looks the right size. Close the top end. Decide whether this is going to be too large or too small and adjust accordingly. Make the largest section first and each smaller one 20% less in width and depth. For each tieback, cut two 2.5 meters (2¾ yards) of cord, fold in half and tie the ends into a knot.

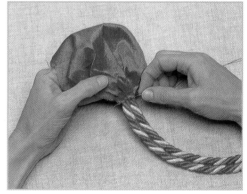

I Cut three pieces of fabric the same size as the model described above. Join the short ends. Press both raw edges under 1.5 cm (⅝ in). Run a gathering thread around the bottom of each section, using double or buttonhole thread. Pull up the gathering thread at the bottom of the largest section and secure.

2 Stuff to make a ball that flattens to a good, even, 'ring' shape as you twist the top tightly. Secure the fabric by wrapping double or buttonhole thread tightly around, as close to the stuffing as possible. Double stitch the top securely. Slip top of this bottom section into bottom of middle one. Pull the gathering threads of middle section tightly and stitch the two 'rings' together. Stuff, then close the top as before.

3 Run a gathering thread around top of top section and stitch knotted ends of the tieback cords securely inside it. Pull up the gathers and secure. Stuff, then pull up the gathering stitches at the bottom and close over the middle section as before. Stitch a key tassel to the bottom of the bell.

Shades

Unless you have the most tremendous view, a real focal point of your room, light entering through any window is improved if it is filtered or controlled. There is a lot to be said for directing daylight to enter the room low, which shades can do very successfully. To test this theory, sacrifice the sky, partly cover the top of a window for a couple of days and notice how much softer the light is and how different the room looks. If you eat or work close to a sunny window, shades can make life much more comfortable. As the sun moves around, they can be raised and lowered by small degrees and with minimum fuss, individually or all at the same time.

Left Here the Roman shade is padded and used instead of curtains for early evening, allowing the radiator to heat the room. Once the room is warmed or a fire is lit, the curtains can be pulled over. The shade should be fitted right up behind the pole, so you may need to block the pole brackets out from the wall to accommodate the thickness of materials.

When to use shades

If you have a radiator underneath a window, shades are fairly essential coverings. Fitted with or without curtains, shades allow the radiator to function efficiently in cold weather. Padded shades covering the whole window and sitting on, or just in front of, the sill are almost as effective as heavy curtains.

Perhaps the most important consideration when choosing shades has to do with personality. You can't guarantee that any shade will pull up straight every time, but if a bit of untidiness does not bother you, then even the most informal shades are fine. If you are anxious about straight lines and matching hems, avoid making shades altogether. Look at the commercial and conservatory possibilities of bamboo, punched metal and split cane and buy only the best, with superior fittings.

Fabrics for shades

Shades need little material, so it's not too difficult to construct a convincing argument for selecting the most extravagant fabric. However, the choices and decisions are really the same as for curtains. Lightly lined or unlined fabrics allow the light to filter through and also direct the light into a room at a low angle. Heavy fabrics are more effective in keeping out cold, and dark colors are better to block light out completely.

Very sheer fabrics, such as organdy, silk, muslin and lace can be used for feminine rooms such as boudoirs, bedrooms and dressing rooms. But don't use these unless you enjoy neatly hand stitching, as both machined lines and uneven hand stitching look ugly on very fine fabrics.

Left All shades become pictures in their own right when down, so some of the most extravagant and well-drawn fabrics can look stunning. This stylized woven flower pattern would be lost in the folds of curtains but really comes into its own here, surrounded by slubbed silk. The soft hem of rolled shades makes stark geometric designs unsuitable.

Types of shade

Rolled shades take time to furl and unfurl, are very informal and soften hard windows. I prefer to see the roll and the ties in a different fabric than that used for the front; it could be a contrasted plain, a change of tone or one pattern with another.

Roman shades are more formal, as each pleat is held straight with a metal or wooden rod behind. Unless you are very keen, avoid using them on windows which are either very high or very wide. It's not that a Roman shade won't look good, but the extremes put pressure on the system and eventually it will be more likely to bend or misfunction.

The design of cascade shades falls between rolled and Roman. Softer in the window, there are no rods, except the lowest one which holds the shape. The same ring and cord mechanism as the Roman shade makes a cascade easier to operate than a rolled shade.

Roller shades are ugly if used alone in a window; the fittings are not attractive and they can't fit close to the sides of the window recess. But they are flat and operate easily, fulfilling the twin criteria of filtering and directing with impunity.

Right Roller shades are the best to use if you want the shade for color or pattern at night, for draft proofing or to control the sunlight but wish them to take up little room when not in use. The fittings can be ugly, so if they are not hidden behind curtains as they are here, make a small valance in the same fabric to fit in front.

Right Used to filter the sunlight and to fully cover the window at night, this shade is made in the same way as a rolled shade — with a little extra fullness across the width, but with rings and cords stitched in place as for a Roman shade.

If the hanging shade falls inwards at the bottom, cut a wooden rod the same width as the recess, cover with the same fabric and stitch to the back, 10 cm (4 in) up from the hem. This will add extra weight and structure to the bottom.

Left This door shade is unlined and is bound with a contrast edge. Rows of rings are stitched to the back, with cords threaded through as for a Roman shade. The same fittings allow the shade to operate in a similar but less formal way.

Rolled shades

◀◀ see also ▶▶
Preparations for shades p. 21
Herringbone stitch p. 146

Mitered corners p. 145
Ties p. 152

This is one of those windows where any form of curtain would have been superfluous. With a view to be envied and no one overlooking, the consideration was only to direct the light into the room without taking too much away. As is so often the case, a snippet from a fashion magazine suggested the shiny ties over matte body. Don't make rolled shades more than one width of fabric wide. These shades look their best in multiples, from two at a simple window to eight around a large bay.

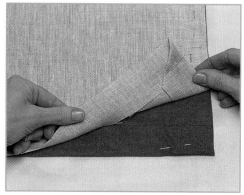

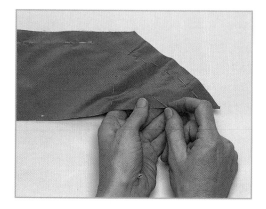

1 Cut fabrics for the shade fronts and cut linings to match. Place the front piece onto a table, right side down, and secure with pins or clamps. Press the sides and hems over 3 cm (1¼ in) and pin. Fold the corner in a half miter. Herringbone stitch all around.

2 Place the lining over, right side up and pin to the front piece. Turn the sides and hem under 3 cm (1¼ in) so that the folds are exactly together. Miter the corners in the opposite direction to the top fabric beneath. Pin folds together and close with ladder or slip stitch.

3 To make the ties, pin the two pieces, fabric and lining, for each tie together with right sides facing. Stitch around, leaving only the top open. Trim the corners, turn right side out and press.

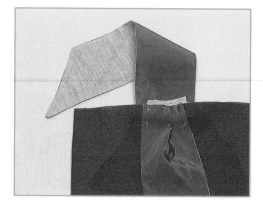

4 Make a small pleat at the top of each tie and pin to the top of the shade, one on the back and one on the front. Stitch to secure. Trim the tops straight. Place the prickly side of some touch and close tape along the top of the front, just covering the raw edges. Keep the ties straight and machine stitch. Press the top of the shade to the back to conceal the tape and stitching. Tack the soft side of the tape to the front of the batten fitted to the wall. Press the shade to the batten, and secure with a tack under each tie. Roll up the bottom and tie the ties.

Opposite Rolled shades can be positioned in a formal, even manner or randomly, each pulled to a different height and none straight. They are perfect for this situation, where daylight needs to be controlled but the windows never completely covered. The view over the city is stunning by day and a great picture of light after dark.

Inset The shades are also attractive to look at from the side, an important consideration when dressing a square bay.

Roman shades

◀◀ see also ▶▶

Rodded shades p. 23   Fittings for shades p. 21
Interlining shades p. 23   Mitered corners p. 145

Roman shades are great for formal situations and minimal rooms where some softness is needed. Stripes and checks look good, but must run straight; fabric with the design or weave running off will not work. Bold designs are effective, but check how the pattern works when the shade is folded. Cut and join fabric and lining. Join widths if necessary. Trim to 12 cm (4¾ in) wider and longer than the finished shade. If you want a padded, interlined shade, cut and join to the same size. Prepare linings as described on page 23.

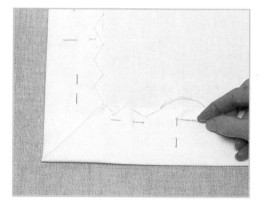

1 Place the shade fabric onto your worktable right side down and secure. Turn over sides and hem by 6 cm (2½ in). Fold the bottom two corners to miter.

2 If interlining, lay the interlining over, unfold the 6 cm (2½ in) and trim interlining along the fold line. Lock stitch the interlining to the fabric at seams, and herringbone all around to secure.

3 Pin the hems and sides and herringbone stitch all around. Leave the mitered folds open.

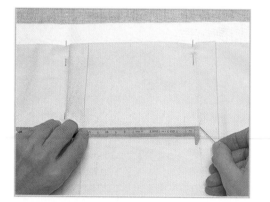

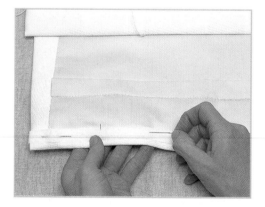

4 Place the prepared lining (see p. 23) over, right side up, matching the sides and hem. Trim the hem to straighten. Score the lining along the folded sides of the shade. Trim along this line. Remove and press sides 3 cm (1¼ in) to the wrong side. Measure up from the hem line to mark the rod pockets with a soft pencil. These must all be exactly straight. Pin the folds in place and stitch. Place the lining back onto the shade, pockets upwards, hems lined up.

5 Pin the sides. Pin each fold in place, checking the measurements to keep the rows parallel. Pin along and across the stitching line. Slip stitch the sides between the pockets. Machine stitch along the pocket lines. Always stitch from the same direction, or the fabrics will ruckle. Measure and mark the overall drop. Trim to 2 cm (¾ in) beyond this line. Fold fabrics to the back. Place a strip of touch and close tape along, just covering the raw edges. Stitch top and bottom.

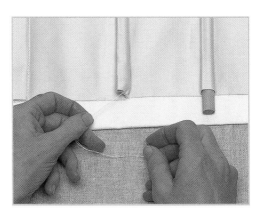

6 Slip the lath into the bottom and one rod into each pocket. Close the pocket ends, miters and hem with slip stitch.

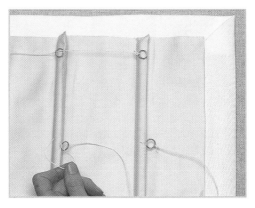

7 Mark the ring positions. Start 5 cm (2 in) from each side and allow three or four rows per width. Stitch the rings firmly in position at the top of the rod pockets. Thread the cords from bottom to top, making sure they are long enough to return to the cord holder. (See p. 21 for fittings for shades.)

Right Roman shades can be operated independently within each window section to work with outside light and inside activity. Stripes look really effective, but they can be difficult to work with unless the fabric is very straight and tightly woven.

Sheers and Lightweights

For years, thin curtains have been looked down on as rather mean and poor, and so they deserved to be. Limp fabrics, more often than not undistinguished in color or design, with machine stitched sides and hems, leave much to be desired. Even conceding a far poorer selection of materials and textiles in the past, I'm not sure why imagination was so lacking at this time. Thick, padded curtains justly became something of a status symbol.

Now, far from being the poor relation, with the most fabulous colors and excitingly adventurous weaves, unlined curtains are back in vogue. As extravagant multi-layers of textiles or just simple sheers, light curtains are a joy.

Individualism has become important again. The revival of the couture dress and the whole media buzz of fashion razzmatazz has made hand stitching and innovative window design not only more sought after, but also more available. In our workshops, we now design and make as many light, unlined curtains as we do heavy, draft-proofing, heat-saving numbers. And more and more often these are used as a second set of curtains, light and fun for summer to replace the more serious, cumbersome winter curtains. And if there isn't the budget for a complete seasonal change, then just one extra, lighter layer to hang behind the winter curtains is an option.

Left The sole function of these curtains is to decorate. They are not needed for warmth or privacy; the fabrics and design were chosen for color and impact alone. The sections of differently colored fabrics have been hand stitched together with tiny, contrast piping between them.

Right White fine linen curtains are ethereal, grounded by the wide border of yellow.

Below For decoration, the border was top stitched into place and embroidery thread was run through. This border was caught under every third stitch, but this may vary according to stitch length, thread thickness and border width.

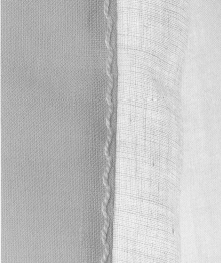

Above A fabric hanging above the bed is made in the same way as any unlined curtain. This one has a bound edge with the striped ticking fabric cut on the cross and ties knotted over small hooks.

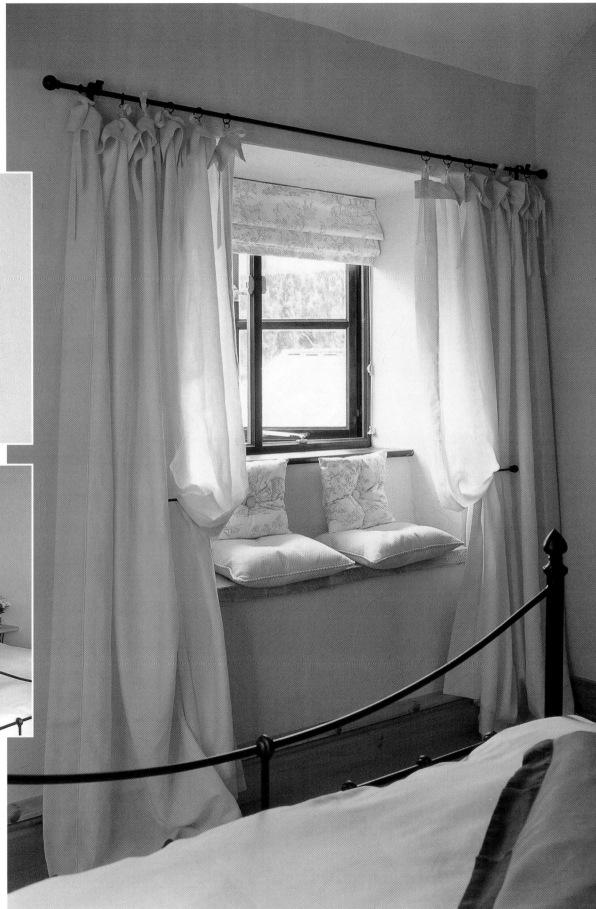

Sheers

Sheers don't stop chilly drafts, they are no good at all if you want to block early morning light and they don't screen out the black and lonely hole of night-time. But they do filter the bright sunlight, which may be lovely to sit in on a spring morning, but which is damaging to furnishings. At the same time, they also provide some privacy. If you like to wake with the light cheering your bedroom, sheer curtains let you do so gradually and calmly. Many sheer fabrics are washable, which is a great bonus, as such light, privacy curtains are often needed in places where they are prone to water damage. Bathroom or bedroom windows, French windows and terrace doors are all subject to condensation. And if they are left open, the curtains can suffer damage from an unexpected wet breeze.

Left One way to hide an unattractive view is with a permanent sheer curtain. The fabric is not at all transparent, but the ochre-toned, printed design filters the light softly. The top is tied to a narrow pole so that the curtain hangs informally and may be pulled back if circumstances require.

Left Curtains in a children's bathroom will inevitably be splashed and touched with sticky fingers. Lightweight cotton voile comes in the most striking colors and can be washed and dried easily. The curtain just pulls on and off a simple wooden pole, held in place with coat hooks.

Right Cotton organdy curtains allow some privacy to a mezzanine floor without blocking off the area and without taking light from the roof window over the main sitting room. The curtains have hand-embroidered detailing, which can be seen on p. 149.

Under curtains

In a cold climate, you will never be able to totally dispense with the thick curtains that insulate a room. Nevertheless, under curtains that can be used for half of the year are a good idea for a new summer look, or simply for a change. Sheer under curtains completely alter the atmosphere of any room, changing the quality of the light flowing in and offering a soft balance to heavy "winter" curtains. Sheer fabric allows light to be filtered and softened rather than blocked out altogether. And, importantly, on a gray day, a white or off-white sheer gives the illusion of much sunnier weather outside than is actually the case. Sheers are wonderful for creating a touch of illusion.

Left Blue silk for cushions and under curtains gives extra depth and color balance to an elegant, monochromatic yellow and off-white room.

Above Fine inset strips of taupe artist's linen have been stitched into the white linen sheer to give visual height. The contrasting textures here are interesting — chintz curtains with a light sheen sit comfortably with the matte and coarser linens.

Above Borders the color of wet sand were chosen to edge off-white linen under curtains. The effect is to soften the aqua-blue check and lead the eye beyond the window to the countryside beyond. Simple embroidery stitches in off-white finish the borders.

Right Fine lampshade silk in the palest ivory offers a lift of color and lightness of texture to traditional toile de Jouy walls and curtains. The edges and hems are finished with tiny rolled hems under creamy picot lace.

Privacy

Unless you are really isolated, bedroom window curtains need to provide some degree of privacy. You can close any curtains or shade to cover the window completely, but then you lose both daylight and view. Light, unlined curtains allow daylight through, while keeping potential prying eyes out. The sheerest fabrics need to be gathered to at least three times fullness, whereas a cotton lawn, for example, might only need minimal, one and a half times fullness.

Left Pleated curtains still need the three times fullness of gathered sheers, but take up less space, hanging as a flat panel. They are especially suitable for a small room or minimalist scheme.

Left Sheer linen and silk fabric printed with beachcombing treasures was the most perfect find for this view. Although these curtains can be closed fully, the need here is to provide just an element of privacy. Two hooks on each curtain allow the panels to slide right back. Slips of colored fabrics echo the varying tones of sea and stones beyond.

Above Fine calico draped in swathes over a pole and falling in bunches onto the floor softens the window and adds a feminine touch.

Fabrics

Many lightweight and open-weave fabrics can be used for sheer curtains. I have used linen scrim (often used to clean windows) and love it. It's a sort of burlap color, so you look straight through it and it's invisible from outside. The fabric does have a couple of drawbacks, which might or might not bother you: the first is that the smell of burlap takes a little while to go away; the second is that cats love to play with the open weave and before you know it, the curtain has been pulled into shreds. Muslin is good; butter muslin if your budget is very tight, the finest quality, which is almost voile, if your budget is better.

Linen and wool are both available very finely woven but with an open weave. Wool looks soft and lovely, but is a bit springy and needs to be over-long to drape well. Linen will take up a great deal of moisture from the window quite happily, but can crease up on the leading edge. Cotton can be woven to almost any specification, from the finest voile to a knitted texture or even open lace work. Organdy and organza are wonderful to look at, but the cotton is a nightmare to iron and the silk rots very quickly. If you want to use either, it's fine, just as long as you know the drawbacks.

If you need a fire-retardant fabric, there are some really good and very convincing polyester voiles which wash in the machine and can be hung back up to dry without ironing. You will probably need to find these through an interior decorator. In any case, always test your proposed fabric for washing, creasing, stitching and so on before using.

Left As long as silk is protected in some way from direct sunlight, it is the best fabric for unlined curtains. From soft silks, such as honan, noil and dupions, to stiff taffetas, its sheen, drape and light reflecting qualities are unmatched.

Layers

Layered fabrics offer more versatility than any other style of curtaining. Three or four layers are fun to work with if you enjoy mixing color, design and texture. All of them can be unlined, or you could add lining to one or two for thickness. There is no reason to make actual use of every layer — you might tie three back for effect and just draw the under one, unless it is a cold evening.

Fabrics

In principle, there is no limit or restriction to the fabrics which you could use. There would be nothing wrong, for example, with a heavy wool or velvet at the front, followed by a cotton stripe, a floral chintz and then a linen sheer. In practice, both budget and house style play major parts in the decision about the layers to choose. As a rule of thumb, go with the style of your house. Thick, heavily textured fabrics absolutely suited to a country house with thick walls and chunky wooden beams are not necessarily going to look good in your house. A fine, architecturally sophisticated house will look best with lightweight and carefully executed fabrics. Of course, while there are no hard and fast rules, you can't choose fabrics at random, either. There needs to be integrity and cohesion, usually achieved with color. You may want to create

Left An utterly feminine treatment for a dressing room. The delicate pink dupion silk allows a lovely warm light into the room, while the fullness is held with fine pin-tucks and the sides and hems are shell stitched. Silk and wool blankets provide warmth for wintertime.

Left Two separate layers of curtaining can be hooked back together or separately. Often the under layer is left to cover the window and the printed curtain is tied back to one side.

a symphony of blues or you may want to recreate the colors in a favorite picture. And always remember scale and proportion — of room, window and the fabrics.

Creasing

Fabrics that crease should be avoided for any curtain that is going to be draped back and let down constantly. The top layer or layers are often kept tied back for the effect of drape, so it really doesn't matter what fabric you choose. However, the layer or layers in use should draw and drop attractively, not look like a dish rag.

Right Antique curtains need to be protected from the sun and under layers are an alternative to the more usual Holland shades. The blue striped cotton middle layer is a foil for the printed pattern and has also been used to edge the under layer. These under curtains are antique embroidered sheets from a French chateau and are tied back separately, so that they can be dropped independently of the other two layers.

Decorating with flowers

Floral decoration is essential to any real home and growing interesting foliage and flowers for cutting is a serious business, whether it be in a country garden or a window box. The flower shops and market stalls on every city street corner are also a serious source of decoration.

Home decorators have long favored rose-strewn chintzes for bedroom and boudoir and for cushions and accessories. Fabric roses at their most basic are pretty simple to make and don't take much time or much fabric. Of course, any flower can be copied, it's just that roses are so easy to make, are loved by everyone and come in every imaginable color.

Left

We designed these very delicate, light curtains to break the potentially heavy atmosphere of a strong attic bedroom that has important beams and stone gable ends and is furnished with tall bookcases and a severe metal bed. As a result, it has now become a room that is loved and enjoyed by every friend and relation who stays in it. Any lightweight fabric can be used in this way, but one which won't crease too much and which has texture to throw the light back from the folds is preferable. Like good architectural detailing, these roses are about the reflected light and shadow created by the shape; there is no need for color or any true form.

There is no formal method for making this sort of decoration — it just develops as you handle the fabric. I concede that just as we are not all natural cooks, neither can we all make magic with fabric. But play with a section of the edge of the curtain in your hand, twisting it loosely and shaping it to resemble rosebuds. Stitch the folds loosely in place — enough to hold but not so much as to constrict the 'bloom'. Make as many or as few as you like, in various sizes and shapes, but don't overdo it. Less is most definitely more in such decoration.

Right

What self-respecting boudoir would be complete without at least one bunch of wonderfully scented, full blown roses on the dressing-table? And if you can't have roses all over the walls, ceilings and curtains in a boudoir, where can you indulge the style? Silk roses look wonderful, throwing the light almost as well as living petals, but any fabric with 'movement' will work — try velvet, fine damasks or silk mixes. Cut lengths of fabric anything from 5 x 25 cm (2 x 10 in) to 25 x 75 cm (10 x 30 in). Fold in half length ways and stitch a running stitch along the ends and one length. Pull up loosely and wind the fabric around to make a tighter or looser 'rose' or 'rosebud.' Tuck the first end in tightly to make a convincing center and wrap the other end under to hide the raw edges. Stitch the shape securely. Cover the raw edges at the back with a folded square of matching fabric and stitch a safety pin or piece of touch and close tape to the back.

A lone gerbera in the garden punctuating flush greenery at the beginning or the end of the season is a fabulous sight. And plain curtaining can surely look lackluster in certain lights or situations. An otherwise inconsequential shot of my garden gave me the inspiration, once again, to borrow ideas from nature. Here a rather dull blue suddenly looks a million dollars when swept back with a precocious, single flower.

To give a lovely touch for a special summer party or wedding, wind real roses round curtains and napkins. Choose the roses for their color and scent; an old-fashioned rose with loose form and a lack of nasty thorns will be less painful to work with and, as a bonus, will drop a perfumed petal carpet for days. Wrap a piece of muslin or a length of the same fabric around the curtain first to prevent the fabric marking. Or stitch the flowers to a sash of something completely different — wide ribbon, folded napkins or a complementary fabric, for example — and pin the ends together at the back of the curtain.

Opposite A tight budget has always been the mother of invention and, indeed, all successful budgeting demands some sacrifice. These curtains, made from a factory length of cotton poplin, cost nothing, and, truth be said, didn't look much either. A circlet of roses saved the day, introducing a little color and providing the means for the lavish drape.

Making unlined curtains

◀◀ see also ▶▶

Preparation for sewing p. 16 | Slip stitch p. 146
Mitered corners p. 145 | Headings p. 62

Preparation: Place the cut and joined fabric (see p. 16) onto your worktable face down. Line up the leading edge with one long side of the table and the hem with one short side of the table. Sweep your meter rule or yardstick over the fabric to remove any rucks. Use an iron to press the fabric to remove all creases and pin or clamp the fabric firmly to the table in three or four places.

1 Turn in the side edge 6 cm (2¼ in) or double the size you want the finished fold to be.

Finger press or press it lightly with an iron. Fold under and in half. Press lightly and pin in place.

2 Turn up the hem 10 cm (4 in) or double the finished hem size. Press lightly, then fold in half to make a double hem. Pin and press. Move the curtain across the table and work on the other side to bring it to the same stage.

3 For anything other than the sheerest fabric, miter the corners as shown and also refer to page 145.

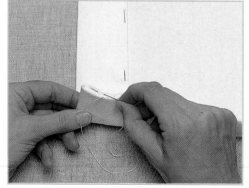

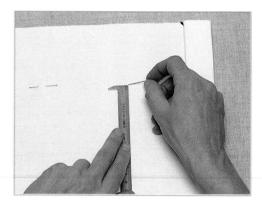

4 If you are using penny weights, slip one into the hem at each corner and seam. Secure with a couple of stitches inside the hem. If using lightweight chain, open up the hem, lie it along the fold and catch to seams and corners.

5 Slip stitch sides and hem, sliding the needle along the inside of the fold between stitches to keep the thread invisible. Ladder stitch the folded edges together at the corners along the miter.

6 Measure from the hem and mark the hook drop of the finished curtain. Measure at 30 cm (12 in) intervals all the way across the curtain. Mark with a row of pins. If you know the overall drop, mark this also. You are now ready to make your chosen heading.

Antique hemp and cotton or hemp and linen sheets from rural France and from middle Europe make good, hard-wearing curtains. As they are already hemmed and seamed with the tiniest of hand stitches, little needs to be done for an informal window treatment. Unlined curtains can be used with any type of shades, either as an extra layer of cover or to soften the edges of the window recess.

Hems and side seams

It is almost easier to work a decorative edging with stitches designed to show than it is to sweat over invisible stitching. So your sole reference is an unhappy memory of a stitched project at elementary school? Think again: the motivation is quite different now and the old basic stitches might well become familiar. If you are a competent sewer, designing stitch combinations could become quite a challenge — and there are books available that clearly list numerous stitches. Adjust the width of the sides and hems to suit your choice of stitches. Check size, space and technique on a scrap of fabric and then begin on the return edge; this gives you some chance to perfect your technique before you move on to the leading edge and hem.

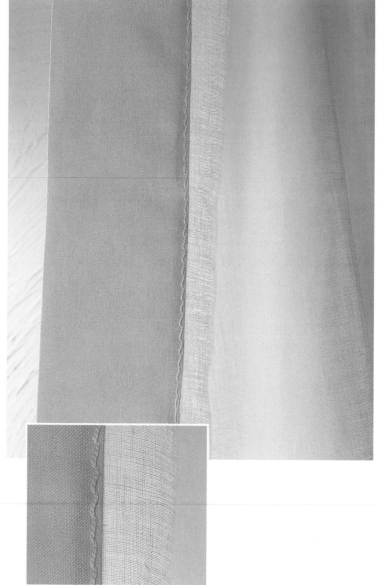

Single chain stitch. This is just a simple variation on age-old chain stitch. Thread a needle with perle or three strands of embroidery thread. Make a single chain stitch on the front, then slide the needle through the folded edge so that the linking thread doesn't show through.

Wave stitch. This is a great way to disguise machine stitching. Machine the hem or seam with the longest stitch, then thread a needle with perle or three skeins of embroidery thread and wind from right to left through every other stitch by hand. It couldn't be easier.

French knots. Make two close together, leave a gap and make another two. The thickness of thread and spacing will vary to suit your fabric. Just bear in mind that if you place them too far apart the hem will bag open and if they are too close together the whole could lose its charm.

This stitch is actually decorating a border already stitched to the curtain, but it could be used just as well to hold a hem and side in place. Herringbone stitch with an added twist. I think 3–4 cm (1⅛ – 1⅜ in) is about the longest the stitch could be; you can make this one as small as you like.

Headings

Gathers

Headings may be gathered for function — as a vehicle to take up fullness — or for decoration — for the effect the frill can make. The hook drop will be calculated from the fitting used, although the overall drop will depend on the importance of the heading and on the distance of ceiling, pole and track above the hook. Take the overall drop from the top of the track, or from just under the pole if the gathering is to be unobtrusive. If there is a frill, check the depth and make the top of the frill the overall drop. Allow the depth of the frill, plus twice the gather depth, for the cut length. If you want to add ties, they need to be stitched in place at the same time as the heading tape. Pin in position and stitch over at least twice to secure.

Ruches

If you can have a fixed heading and plenty of fabric fullness, you might decide to ruche the heading onto a pole, making a frill above. This is also the way to make the heading and pocket for net curtains if you want to use the old fashioned wire fitting or a tension rod. For a wire, a 2 cm (¾ in) frill and a 2 cm (¾ in) pocket is usually sufficient.

Find the circumference of the pole and decide how much of a frill you want to create above it. The hook drop in this case will be the bottom of the pole. In order to calculate the overall drop, allow the depth of the frill, plus half the pole circumference, plus 1 cm (⅜ in) for leeway. Then add the same again, plus 2 cm (¾ in) for the cut length.

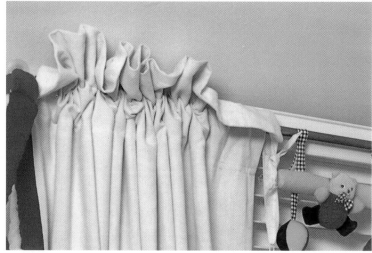

Press the fabric to the back along the overall drop line. Press the hem to the depth of the gathers. Pin. Place heading tape over to just cover the lower edge. Pin and stitch in place. Make and stitch a hook band to cover (see p. 113). And if you prefer to hand stitch the gathers, follow the same method as described for interlined curtains on pages 110 to 113.

Press the fabric to the back of the curtain along the overall drop line. Press 2 cm (¾ in) under and pin. Mark the frill depth. Stitch close to the folded edge, and again along the frill line. Neaten the ends. Thread onto the pole.

Knife pleats

We often use this heading for sheer curtains that fold back behind heavier curtains, as flat pleats take up the least room. Your overall drop will be from the top of a track or bottom of a pole. Allow twice the heading depth for the cut length. You should preplan the exact fullness (see p. 19), but if you decide to work with whatever widths the fabric adds up to, you will need to plan the pleat sizes. Measure the flat width of the curtain and deduct its width when finished. Work out the percentage of fullness and pleat accordingly. Pleated headings tend to 'shrink' as they are stitched, so this little extra allowance can be useful. And even if not used, the slightly wider width is unlikely to be a problem, whereas a too narrow one would be.

Buttonholes

Flat headings are good if you have limited pull-back space either side of the window, or if you really don't want to make the curtaining too dominant where there is already much of visual interest. Some fabrics just need to be seen flat and are completely spoiled if the pattern is distorted with gathers and pleats. The hook drop will be the top of the buttonhole; the overall drop any distance above that. Decide how deep the heading should be in total and add twice that to get the cut length. The number of fittings or buttonholes and the distance between them depends on the width of the curtain to the window and on how the curtain will hang. You may need one fixing each side or several hooks at intervals all the way across.

Press to the back along the overall drop line and fold half up under. Press and tack. To make the pleats, pin in 11 at 3 cm (1¼ in) gaps and make pleats of 2.25 cm (⅞ in), taking 4.5 cm (1¾ in) of fabric. Pin top and bottom. Stitch in place close to the top and close to the fold line. Decorate with embroidery stitches or beads if you wish. Hand stitch hooks behind to make a small hook band (see page 113).

Press fabric to the wrong side along the overall drop line. Fold under in half and press. Stitch just half a centimeter (about quarter of an inch) from the fold line and from the top to secure. Mark the buttonhole positions with crossed pins and make buttonholes as shown on page 147.

Bindings and borders

Bindings and borders are chosen as much to add another color or pattern to the main fabric as to finish the edges. Sometimes, short curtains are the best choice, for example, when a radiator or a piece of furniture has to stay just below the window, making long curtains impossible. I prefer to define short curtains with a narrow edging — at least those that hang just in front of a window sill.

Whether the curtains are short or long, a bought braid or fan edging can be effective. But if you want to use fabric, choose one that will complement the main curtain and not overpower it. If you use a plain fabric with a printed cotton, choose a middle tone from the colors. If in doubt, check the colored dots on the selvage that show the breakdown of colors used in printing the cloth. The softer colors will melt away, the strongest demand

Right An inset taupe strip defines a border that is made from the same fabric as the main curtain.

Below left The checked border, woven in deeper tones of the same colors, echoes and complements the design of the main fabric.

Below right A wide border in a contrasting color acts as a frame to plain curtains.

Above The impact of a deep border in a strong color is softened by the inset strips inserted close by. Another inset strip defines the smaller bordered hem of the under curtain.

Right Two different striped fabrics in the same colors and from the same collection as the floral print have been cut into strips to make elaborate borders on sides and hems and a simpler edge to the heading.

too much attention, but mid-tones add another dimension to the finished window.

If you are happy to be more adventurous, mix a striped or checked border with a printed design, or a stripe border with a checked curtain — or tiny rosebuds with overblown roses. The possible combinations are endless. Just remember the balance of scale, keep to one main color and similar textures, and you won't go far wrong.

If you are using plain colors only, try a white border with natural linen curtains for a subtle effect, or bright yellow or sky blue with white for a splash of drama. With care and attention to the tonal value of the different cloths, many interesting combinations can be created — bronze and leaf green, red with tan, black and white, gray and chocolate, mauve and ginger, ivory and rose, to suggest a few. Take your inspiration from the fashion world, or from a painting, to be sure of your combinations.

A border or binding can be useful when the pattern repeat of a fabric fits exactly into the space before the heading and hem allowance has been included, especially if the fabric has a long repeat or is on the expensive side. Deep borders help if you are short of fabric, whether by accident or design, or if you need to move existing curtains to a taller window, perhaps when you move house.

Far left A bright ochre glazed cotton edges blue and white gingham. The strong contrast settles the small curtains against the granite sill and works equally well with the green outdoors.

Left The lining of this reversible fabric has been folded to the front and stitched neatly to give the effect of a border.

Opposite Instead of adding a border to the main curtains, the checked lining has been brought to the front and stitched to give the same effect. The blue and white checked border stitched to the shower curtain has been made to the same size as the curtain edging.

Kitchen gingham with bindings

When I designed this kitchen, I wanted its colors and style to be sturdy and traditional to work well with the natural world outside, as this house is situated deep in the countryside. For the curtains, I chose blue and white, which must be the most traditional of color combinations, and cotton gingham check for purity and simplicity. The yellow bindings and tiebacks — and the floor tiles — add bite and complement and highlight the greens and blue-greens of the kitchen cupboards.

Preparation: For a binding 1.5 cm (⅝ in) wide when finished, you will need to cut strips of 6 cm (2⅜ in), joined on the cross. Curtains will be cut to size and joined with French or flat and fell seams. Place the curtain onto the worktable, with the right side up. Line up the leading edge along one long side and the hem along one short side. Check the measure of the overall drop and trim away any excess. Pin or clamp the curtain to the table.

Above Ticking stripes and gingham checks have been woven for centuries and still look best in country situations — especially in bedrooms and kitchens.

Right A simple door shade was edged in the same yellow glazed cotton binding.

◀◀ see also ▶▶

Borders and bindings p. 151
Preparations for shades p.

21

Stitches p. 146

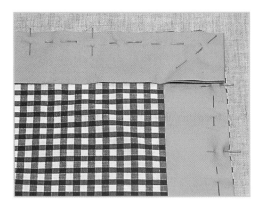

1 Start pinning the edging strip on approximately 20 cm (8 in) from the heading on the return side, the least visible spot for the join. With the right sides together, pin the binding along to the corner. At the corner, fold the binding away from the curtain at a right angle. Finger press, fold it back down along the heading side, making a triangular flap. Secure, and carry on pinning along this next side. Repeat with the next three corners and sides.

2 Make the join, machine stitching the two pieces together across the width. Stitch the binding in place, keeping the distance from the raw edge 1.4 cm (½ in). Stop stitching 1.4 cm (½ in) from each corner and reverse stitch to secure. Lift the needle up, turn the curtain, fold the flap back and recommence 1.4 cm (½ in) from the corner and next side. The needle should go back in right next to the last stitch for a really neat corner. Press the binding away from the curtain.

3 Fold behind, holding the binding tight against the edge of the curtain for a neat, strong edge. (If you have made an error, just make sure the binding is the same width all around.) The corners should fall into neat miters at the front. Press and pin from the front, leaving the corners.

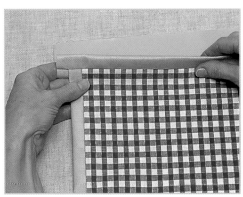

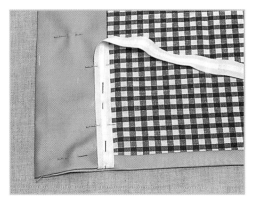

4 Turn the curtain over. Fold the binding in half — the fold line should just cover the stitching line — and pin. To neaten the corners, press the flap in the opposite direction to the front. Snip 1.5 cm (⅝ in) into the binding, so that the first side will fold under. Fold the adjacent side under. Pin. Slip stitch all round, catching into the machine stitches so no stitching is visible from the front and the machined line is covered. Use the smallest of stitches.

5 Cut the heading binding the width of the finished curtain, plus 2 cm (¾ in) for each side. Add the depth of the finished frill plus 5 cm (2 in). Stitch to the curtain with right sides facing, allowing the same measurement from the raw edges. Press the binding to the back.

6 Turn the raw edges in and pin. Pin the heading tape on, covering the raw edge. Stitch in place. This method gives a firmer heading. If this isn't necessary, just bind the top in the same way as the other three sides.

Hook-back curtain

◀◀ see also ▶▶
Bordering a corner p. 151
Buttonhole stitch p. 147

It is not always possible to match checks and stripes at each corner. To do so, the checks need to be symmetrical (which they often aren't) and the curtain length and width planned accordingly. As long as everything is neat, with angles folded evenly, a perfect match is often unnecessary.

Preparation: The widths of the border can be varied around the panel. Here the heading is narrower than the sides and hem. To keep the checks in line, make each side separately and join with flat seams.

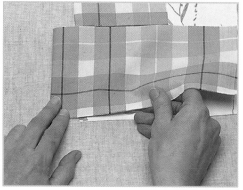

1 With right sides together and starting 5 cm (2 in) from the most inconspicuous corner, pin the border to main fabric 1.5 cm (⅝ in) from raw edges. Stop 1.5 cm (⅝ in) from the corner and fold fabric 45° back on itself. If using a check or stripe, follow weave to keep the border straight.

2 Measuring from pinned seam line, mark border width and fold it right back on itself so that raw edges line up with the next side. Pin across angle to hold in place. Repeat for next three corners. Just past the last, join border ends with a flat seam and press.

3 Stitch border to main fabric 1.5 cm (⅝ in) from edge. Stop 1.5 cm (⅝ in) from end of each corner. Fold flap back and pin to mark the last stitch. Start at pin and continue along next side. From front, press border away from main fabric. Miter corners and finger fold border to back.

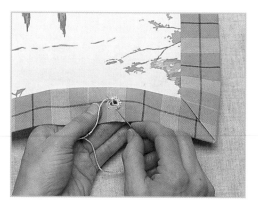

4 Turn over and press along the folded edge. Press the seam allowance under 1.5 cm (⅝ in) so that the machined stitches are just covered. Make a 1.5 cm (⅝ in) snip into the border in line with the stitching on the adjacent side. Open out the corner and fold over to make a miter.

5 Fold the other sides under and make corners in the same way. Slip stitch all around and press. Fold the panel as it will be when it is hooked back and mark the four or five hole positions. Cut holes and neaten all around with buttonhole stitches.

Facing page I wanted to introduce fabric into this conservatory to minimize the dark outside at night and to soften the intense heat of summer. Even sheer voiles were too fussy for this room, and I didn't want to cover all the windows. The checked border acts as a frame to a fabric which is like a painting, with its delicate pattern and traditional ochre coloring. Hand-stitched button-holes hold the curtain onto basic cup hooks to cover the window or to fold back to the sides.

Pleats and pin-tucks

I first saw pleated hems some years ago as I was walking past the Paris showroom of the French designer Agnès Comar. It was an idea so original but so obvious that I found myself wishing, in frustration, that I'd thought of it first.

Pin-tucks take up the fullness in a feminine, yet neat and controlled, way but allow maximum light to filter through. They fit well in a bathroom or dressing-room window where privacy is essential. An extravagant window design with several layers is always lovely, but it can be cumbersome and unsuitable for some situations and for many small windows. Pleating and pin-tucking are lovely ways to use the fullness of one or two of the curtains in a multi-layered design. A flat fabric with intricate stitching is so much prettier and softer than a roller shade, which so often seems the only option in a small space.

Almost any lightweight textile is suitable for pleats or pin-tucks. One which will finger press will be easiest to work with when it comes to planning and preparing the pleats. Unless a pattern, whether woven or printed, fits in with the size pleats you want, resist using it, as it could look skewed when you've pleated it. A woven fabric may also be unsuitable as it may be too bulky to form properly crisp pleats.

For light under curtains, I tend to use linen voile, cotton organdy, silk organza, cotton lawn, silk habutai, taffeta and, occasionally, a fine wool challis (although it's springy and needs a bit of a fight if you are to form flat pleats). Horizontal pleats could be stitched into almost any fabric, but again I favor plain weaves, preferring the design and shadow play created by the work itself to shine through without the distraction of pattern.

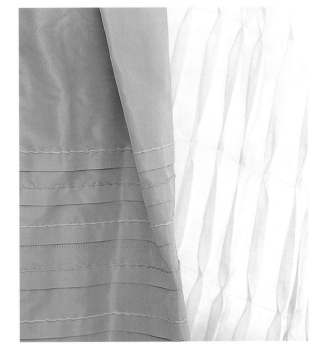

Pin-tucks and pleats together might seem extravagant, but in plain fabrics the contrasting textures are emphasized.

The folds and shadows of deep pleats give interest to plain fabric and weight and shape to the hems of light fabrics.

Understated elegance

◀◀ see also ▶▶
Headings p. 62
Layers p. 52
Pin-tucks p. 77

I'm really pleased with this window; I love the contrast of vertical and horizontal pleats, the way the light filters through and the gentle, neutral coloring of the whole room. Since my first experiment, I have played with many variations, sometimes making cascades of small pleats and at others three or four very deep pleats from the waist down. Pleating makes a simple unlined curtain look a million dollars.

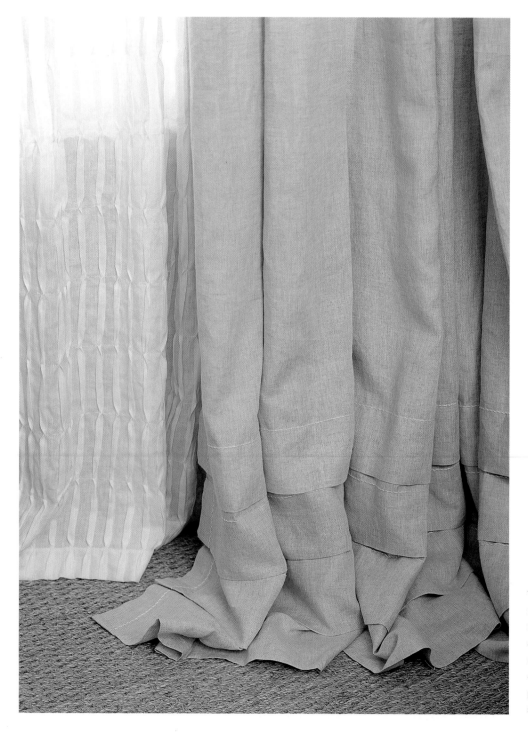

Preparation: I think it's best to make a model to begin with, so that you really know how the finished result will look, and to make sure you order enough fabric. Any old sheet, a piece of curtain lining or length of muslin will do. Draw or sketch the pleating arrangement that you think will work best for your window. Don't be afraid to exaggerate: if the pleats are too mean and too far apart, they will look abandoned. Unless you have deliberately devised a design involving many pleats of equal size, always make them deeper towards the hem. If you would like a starting suggestion, try five pleats: the first 7 cm (2¾ in), needing 14 cm (5½ in) of fabric, overlapping the next and graduated until 18 cm (7 in), that is 36 cm (14 in) of fabric. The hem should be double and finish at the top of the last pleat to avoid an extra 'line'. Adjust the pleats as you wish until the length and balance is right.

White and taupe together create cool, elegant rooms. Flooring, walls, bed linen and curtain fabrics in natural materials and colors provide a restful and calm environment. The headboard has been upholstered in a stunning fabric with a brilliantly colored and stylized flower design, while pleats and pin-tucks transform plain fabrics into intricate and sophisticated panels.

Pin-tucked linen curtain

◀◀ **see also** ▶▶
Linen p. 8   Borders and bindings p. 151
Curtain poles p. 25

Tea-towelling linen and satin ribbons soften the window and frame the view from a light, airy attic studio. I chose the linen for its weave, but mainly because it is so rewarding to work with. Pleats like to be finger pressed into shape and don't bounce out as soon as you turn your back. You still need to be very precise with measurements and stitching, as you must keep the pleats exactly parallel.

Pin-tucks are really just that — pin sized — fine for small girls and wedding dresses, but unrealistic for a large curtain. You must also consider balance and scale; the size of the tucks must be appropriate for your window and room. The pleats in the curtains here form a slight scalloped shape at the lowest point. You can easily do something similar, but equal lengths are fine.

Pin-tucks are light and delicate and need correspondingly light and delicate fabrics and trimmings. The ribboned tied headings are hooked onto a fine steel pole and decorated with frosted glass drops. The pin-tucks are pressed flat after stitching, but it doesn't matter if they become wavy with time.

Preparation: Allow pleats of 1.25 cm (½ in) finished, needing 2.5 cm (1 in) of fabric, with 2.5 cm (1 in) gaps between. Either make a model or work out mathematically the exact width the curtain will need to be before the pleats are stitched in place. Cut and join accordingly. Pleats and tucks have a tendency to 'walk' as they proceed along the width. Before you start, you might like to make a few of marks where you expect (say) every tenth pleat to eventually be. Tack down the whole length of the center of the pleats, starting with the center of the curtain. When you later arrive at these marker points, you can then make the small adjustments necessary to keep you on course.

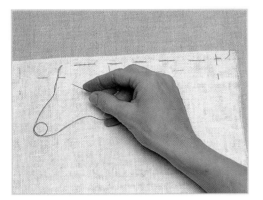

1 Start at the center and work out to each side. Press the curtain in half and pin in the first tuck. Use enough pins and position them so that they don't all fall out as the fabric is moved. Or tack the tucks instead.

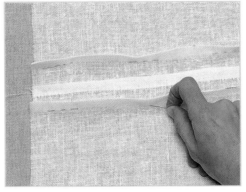

2 Stitch the first (center) tuck to give yourself an accurate measuring point. Measure from the center of the first tuck to the center of the next tuck. Mark the length. Press along this line. Pin or tack the tuck size. Continue until all tucks are in place.

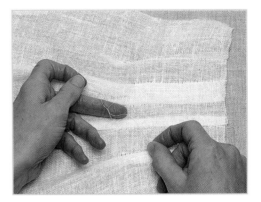

3 Stitch the tucks, finishing off at the bottom with just one double stitch. Turn the work to the inside. Pull the threads through and tie in a tight knot. Cut the ends off.

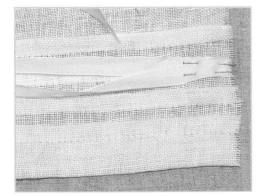

4 Press the pleats all in the same direction. Fold the ribbon ties in half and align the fold to the raw edge. Stitch the ribbon ties in place. Secure with at least two rows of stitching.

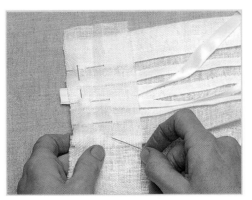

5 Bind the top edge with a self binding to neaten. Cut the width of the finished curtain plus 2 cm (¾ in) for each end by 8 cm (3 in) for a 2 cm (¾ in) finished binding. Stitch to the front, 2 cm (¾ in) from the raw edges.

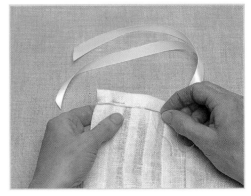

6 Press to the back, fold under 2 cm (¾ in) and slip stitch to close.

Lined
Curtains

Curtains are lined for both practicality and appearance. Perhaps the most important of the practical reasons for lining curtains is to save the main fabric from the ravages of sunlight, which will rot and fade them in a surprisingly short time, especially at a south facing window with an open exposure. Condensation can also damage curtain fabric very quickly, and lining will prevent moisture from getting through to the top fabric. Lining is also chosen to enhance the look of the curtain fabric, backing it to deepen the colors, to add a little bulk or even to do both at the same time.

Choosing lining material

Sateen curtain lining is a treated fabric designed for the express purpose of lining curtains so must be considered the best line of defense if you foresee a practical problem, such as exposure to sunlight or damp. It is worth checking with your supplier that you have found the best quality lining, even if your choice needs to be ordered specially. It is false economy to compromise, so ask to see several samples of varying weights and weaves. The difference between the least and the most expensive available will be immediately obvious.

Most linings will need to be replaced after a minimum of ten, and probably a maximum of fifteen, years. You might be able to clean up general wear and tear, but any areas fragile from direct sunlight will be weakened still more during any cleaning process. Watermarks probably won't come out completely and neither will fly spots. It seems that small puppies like to christen the backs of curtains;

Above Dark linings should usually be avoided, unless, as here, the window is set into a deep recess. The strong red is not apparent from the outside and there is little chance of fading from direct sunlight.

Left Wide stripes suit cottage style homes in which contemporary art and sculpture are collected and displayed. The fold-over heading tabs were made and buttoned with the alternate colors. Tabbed headings are only really feasible where you can reach the top of the curtains to pull them by hand.

Above left Double layers of lined curtains may be used together or separately, depending on the occasion and the time of year.

Left A narrow brass tube held on coat hooks provides the hanging method in a small window where there is no room for elaborate fittings. It has been painted blue to blend in with the checked curtains.

Above The heading stays in position while the curtain is hooked back to one side to show an equally respectable lining. When more privacy is required, it is an easy matter to release the corner, letting the curtain drop over the window.

neither aroma nor stain will clean out successfully unless done immediately and professionally.

Basic lining material is made in several tones of neutral — from white to ivory, cream or ecru. One of these will best suit the ground of your chosen fabric. When making your color choice, bear in mind the façade of your house. The right color can complement painted rendering or any natural stonework and, conversely, the wrong color can detract from the overall look of the house. Aim to choose linings that will enhance the outside and keep them all the same. The colors and shapes showing at the windows should never compromise the architecture of a building.

Decorative linings

Without interlining, patterned or colorful linings will almost undoubtedly show through at some time or another. Checks and stripes are interesting, but just check that any faint shadow of pattern doesn't disturb the appearance of the front of the fabric. Kitchens, hallways or doors are good places to have interesting linings, which could be thicker than the front fabric if drafts are an issue.

Layers

Where a multi-layered design has been chosen, at least one of the layers should be lined. If not to give some soft bulk, then almost certainly lining is needed to prevent the layers being seen together. I usually line the top layer in something insignificant, to make sure the colors remain true, and I line inner layers if I want each fabric to be visible in its own right. Of course, there are many times when layers are chosen with the sole intention that the various colors and tones will interact with each other, so that the whole effect depends on this chemistry. You could still line the undermost layer with a fine lawn, light enough that daylight is barely filtered — the effect will remain unspoiled and all the fabrics will be protected.

Left Blue and white ticking stripes for border and linings complement summer flowers.

Opposite Layers of shimmering silks — three in all, used together or separately — make an exciting contrast with the sturdy oak furniture.

Below These curtains remain closed at the top and drape back, so the lining is at least as important as the top fabric.

Making lined curtains

◀◀ see also ▶▶
Making curtain linings p. 17   Lock stitch p. 147
Mitered corners p. 145

Preparation: Cut and join fabric and lining widths as necessary. Place the fabric face down onto your worktable. Line up the leading edge along one long side and the hem along one short side of the table. The curtain is most likely to be wider than your worktable, so leave the excess dropping over the side while you work on the section on the table. Sweep your meter rule or yardstick over the fabric to remove every ruck; clamp or pin to the table. Press to remove any creases.

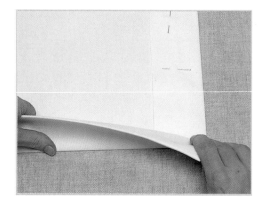

1 Fold the side over 6 cm (2½ in); finger press and pin. Fold up the hem 16 cm (6½ in) and press lightly. Open out the fold and refold in half, making an 8 cm (3¼ in) double hem. Press very lightly. You want the fabric to stay put, but not with a sharply pressed edge.

2 Miter the corner with a long miter. If the fabric you are using is very light in color, cut away the corner of the triangle so that there is one less layer. Hold the fabric up to the light so that you can assess the effect of the folded layers on the fabric color.

4 Herringbone the sides in place, close the miter with small ladder stitches and slip stitch the hem. If you can, adjust your stitch length so the caught threads are almost invisible in a weave or pattern detail. Move the curtain across the table and bring the other half to the same stage.

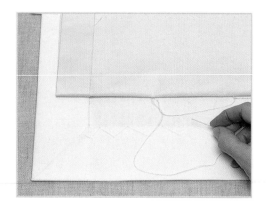

5 Place the lining over the curtain, wrong side down, matching seams and hemlines. Smooth out any rucks and creases. You need to lock stitch the lining to the curtain fabric along the length. To do this, fold the lining back on itself at the first seam and stitch together, starting and finishing approximately 10 cm (4 in) from heading and hem.

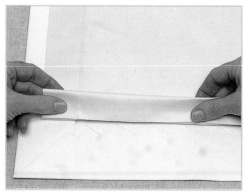

6 Fold the lining back flat, smooth out; lock together again halfway across the width. Fold the lining flat again, score along the folded curtain side and trim away excess. Turn under 3 cm (1¼ in), showing 3 cm (1¼ in) of the curtain fabric. Finger press and pin. Bring the rest of the curtain to the same stage.

3 If you are using penny weights, insert one into each corner and seam. Secure inside the hem with a couple of stitches. Or lie light chain weight inside the hemline and stitch at each corner and seam. Pin.

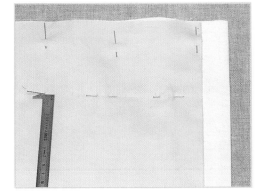

7 Measure from hem to mark hook drop across the curtain every 30 cm (12 in); pin on this line to hold the fabrics together securely. Slip stitch the lining in place at each side from hook drop to hem, and then about 8 cm (3¼ in) along the hem. Make a stitched bar at each seam. Turn the curtain to place heading along the long side of the table; you can now work on the whole curtain. Once you are sure of the overall drop, measure from the hook drop and mark again with a row of pins. Make your chosen heading.

Linings protect the main fabric from sunlight and general wear and tear. Expect to change linings before the whole curtains — after ten or twelve years in a rural location and five or six in town.

Headings

Formal headings

Always stiffen formal headings with buckram, cotton heading tape or dressmaker's interfacing. Buckram should be used to hold formal pleated headings firmly, and cotton tape or dressmaker's interfacing for a softer finish. If you have decided to line your curtains, you will need to strengthen the headings to show some form. This technique is quite different to that used for heading sheer curtains; although they are made up similarly, they can remain soft and drop a bit within the spirit of the whole look. Stitch the top of the stiffening to the pressed overall drop line with herringbone stitches (see p. 146). Fold the heading back over and pleat up as planned.

The most usual pleats are triple or double pleats, goblets, inverted or box pleats, all of which are explained in detail for interlined curtains on pages 110-11. You can follow exactly the same instruction for lined curtains. Use whatever spacing and depth best suits your window.

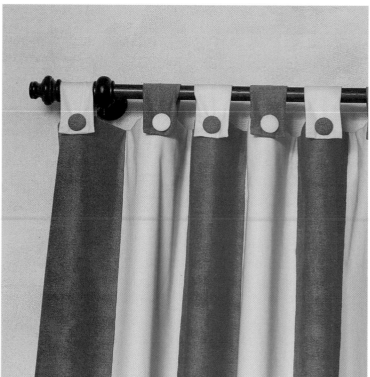

Goblet

French or triple

Tabbed

Informal headings

Gathering lined curtains is very much the same process as it is for all other curtains, whether unlined or interlined (see pages 62 and 112-114). With lined curtains, just don't cut the lining away at the overall drop line — you can fold it down with the curtain fabric. Make up the lining and fabric as one — and if you are using a fine fabric, the extra weight is quite helpful. If you are using bought tape to make the frilled or bunched heading, no extra stiffening is needed apart from this extra lining. Hand gathering needs to be supported a bit more, so stitch an extra piece of heading tape in-between the linings before you make the gathering stitches.

If you don't need to pull the curtains back away from the window, the headings can be fixed in place. One way to do this is to make a pocket that threads the curtain over a metal or wood pole. The pocket should be bigger than the diameter of the pole. If you want a tightly gathered frill, allow just 1 cm (½ in). If you want to use less fullness, or if your fabric is already quite heavy, a deeper pocket, double the diameter of the pole, will look better. You don't need a frill above — the curtain could just thread through, especially if the fabric is thick, not full, and if the pocket is deep. The making of this ruched heading is described on page 62 (consider lining and fabric as one).

Bunched headings are good for lined curtains if you want the headings to be soft, but full. On pages 116-7, there are instructions for bunched headings on interlined curtains. The basic method is the same if your fabric is of medium to heavy weight. If it is quite fine, you might like to stitch a layer of light or medium weight interlining into the whole of the heading. This extra body will make the headings puffier. Three times fullness, instead of the usual two and a quarter to two and a half, will also give you more fabric to scrunch up.

Ruched

Gathered

Attached valances

The process is the same for making a valance that is attached either to unlined curtains or interlined curtains. Interlined curtains become very heavy to handle and the headings bulky. You will probably not be able to machine any heading through all of the layers, so be prepared to hand stitch pleats or gathers. And unlined curtains will carry an attached valance as long as you stiffen the heading sufficiently between the main curtain and the valance.

You can choose any headings to go with an attached valance — gathered or bunched for informality; triple, goblet or inverted pleats for a more formal window; tabbed or ruched if the headings are fixed. Stitch fringe or any bought edge to the bottom of the valance once it is attached. The curtains are heavy enough to work without the additional weight of fringe.

When and where to use

Choose attached valances to redress visual balance — to break the height of a tall window, for example, or to balance floor-length curtains with a small window. To raise the top of a window, make fixed headings with an attached valance. Close the headings and tie the curtains back, allowing the attached valance to drop over and cover the dead light. An attached valance can look like a simpler, separate valance. In situations where there is little or no space above the window, you can get the effect of a valance when curtains are closed, without losing light when they are open.

Fabrics and detailing

Any complementary texture and pattern can work, although very often the same fabric as the curtain is the better choice, allowing the detail of design rather than the fabric combination to predominate. If your preference is to mix, consider varying self-colored textures or tones.

Some sort of detail is essential to define the lower edge of the valance, making it obvious where the curtain stops and the valance begins. Fringing is a good way in which to create a change of texture, while an embroidered braid or ribbon can produce an interesting contrast.

Making

Attached valances are stitched to the curtain at the same time as the heading. There can be quite a bulk of fabric to deal with, so make sure that your machine can cope. Or, as we often do, hand stitch the whole lot with long, strong needles and buttonhole thread.

If your curtain is interlined, the valance should have less weight than the curtains or it becomes just too much to handle. You can either just line it, or use a fine domette or sarille as a lighter interlining. Test a piece of each of the fabrics to see how they work together.

Make the valance in the same way as the curtain, but cut away any interlining at the hem to

I rarely use a fabric more than twice, and this is the only time I have also used a similar treatment. The curtains in the bathroom on the right have come from the hallway of a previous house. Here they break all the rules of proportion and balance and yet look really good. The attached valances on the curtains below were chosen to add formality where full valances would have been too elaborate. On a short, wide window the valances and the shade have added much needed visual height.

Right The strong lines effected by a deeper colored border echo and balance the weight of the solid and prevalent ceiling beams. An interesting metal pole introduces a light touch. The bolts in the beams (not shown) are also black metal, part of the traditional structure and character of what was once a cider barn.

Below A neat piped edge between the border and the curtain is an interesting way to introduce the two fabrics.

Above Goblet headings and deep bullion fringe keep these hall curtains formal yet still heavy enough for a country location. The terra cotta tiled floors and oak furniture, as well as the setting of the house, dictated the overall style of informal elegance.

reduce bulk, stitch hem and side, leaving the top. Allow 3 cm (1¼ in) above the overall (finished) drop for both valance and curtain. Pin together the top of the valance and the top of the curtain along the overall drop line, right side of the valance faced to the curtain lining. If you are using a pleated heading, the buckram should be inside already. Stitch 3 cm (1¼ in) from the raw edges. Trim away all excess fabric in layers to avoid it getting too bulky. Fold the valance to the front and press. Make pleats or stitch gathered headings.

Bindings

The way to make bindings for a lined curtain is the same as it is for an unlined curtain. Just lock the lining to the fabric, trim both to exactly the same size, tack together almost at the raw edges and then treat the two fabrics as one. The full instructions are given on pages 68-9.

Color and pattern

I can't bear the sort of edgings that hit you in the eye as soon as you enter the room. If you want to use two plain colors, just keep the tonal harmony and never pick the strongest color in a print for the edging. Tone on tone is fine, as are same colored stripes in varying widths, a small companion to a larger print, and the mid tone of any multi-colored textile. All the details, especially the edges, must be subtle to be appropriate. Binding is quite a formal way to finish off a curtain and as such should remain understated and elegant.

Stripes look very smart and pristine when used to define checks or another stripe. There is no difference here from making a plain binding, but look for tightly woven fabric. If the fabric is too stretchy, you'll have a difficult time pinning it straight in the first place and then stopping the edge waving as you press the binding over.

Fabrics

Fabrics need to be compatible in weight and construction. Shiny and matte, plain with pattern, check with stripe, are all great combinations as long as cotton is with cotton and silk with silk and so on. If in doubt about the compatibility, wash small samples and see how they react. A heavy edge will drag on the curtain, differing weaves will pull against each other in time and flimsy fabrics on heavy curtains need to be very carefully designed.

Piping

If you want to stitch piping to the inside edge of the border, you will need to pin the border on, make the miters, take it off and pipe around the mitered corners. A less fiddly method is to stitch the piping to the curtain. Lock the lining and top fabric to each other, then tack together to hold the edges, but also to mark the stitching line for the piping. Pencil a line as far from the edge as the border width, pin the piping to this line and stitch through all layers. Make the border as usual, stitching to cover the piping stitching line.

Left A cross-piped ticking stripe is a neat way to introduce a much stronger border. Here the red linen border is also the lining. The piping is stitched onto the ticking front 10 cm (4 in) from the edges of sides and hem, the locked-in lining brought to the front, trimmed and hand stitched to the back of the piping.

Opposite A binding is just a decorative way to 'finish' the edge of a curtain. It is also a good way to introduce another tone, another scale or another color. Both the cutting and stitching need to be tackled with great care and patience for a neat result, especially if the binding is cut on the cross.

Patterned borders

Some fabrics are woven or printed with their own borders, which might be perfectly placed, or need to be reorganized. Whether the fabric has a border on both sides or on one side only, the choices are usually the same. It is almost always best to cut the borders off and to then stitch them back on again, which is essential if the border is on one side of the fabric only. Just occasionally, the border pattern runs into the main pattern, but usually there is a distinct cutting line.

You will need to consider how the pattern can be used best to suit your design. For multi-width curtains, you might have enough to edge the heading and/or the hems. Make the sides and hems the priority, then see if you have enough for the heading. If the border came from two sides, you might still have enough to insert between the widths. Or you can use any spare border fabric for valances, tiebacks, or cushion borders.

If you are going to join sides and hem, or sides and heading, always miter the corners and try to make the miter successful — choose the best place and then work from the corner up. If, because of the width and length of the curtain, you can only make one really successful pattern across the miter, choose the most prominent position and the others probably won't show. Or you might be able to trim a few centimeters off the width if you then get two good miters without damaging the fullness. Floral patterned borders are usually more accommodating than geometric ones.

If there is a definite direction to the pattern, the sides will need to run the same way. Start with the leading edge and run the pattern from top to bottom and then along the hem towards the outside edge. Join at this corner, so that the pattern will change direction here.

This neat border gives the impression of a woven braid that has been stitched on — until you look closely. Joining two widths of fabric for each curtain left enough spare printed border to finish the bottom of the valance as well.

I love the way extra and unexpected colors have been introduced into the border alone; if it had also been used on the heading, the curtains would have looked shorter and boxy, so this lighter treatment was devised.

Making

The options are:

• Border on both sides and along the hem.
Join the curtain widths. Stitch the border around in one length, mitering the corners carefully. Take account of any directional pattern.

• Border all around.
Join the curtain widths. Stitch the border all around, making the heading and leading edge miter the priorities.

• Border on sides only.
Join the curtain widths. Stitch the borders back to each side, keeping the direction of pattern the same.

• Border on leading edges and hems.
Join the curtain widths. Stitch the border around, starting at the top of the leading edge and working down, moving to the outer edge.

• Border all around and between widths.
Join the curtain widths, with one row of the border between each. Then make the outer border in one, starting at the top of the leading edge.

• Border on hem only.
Join the curtain widths. Stitch the border to the hem. You could stitch several rows of borders in succession, with or without some of the main fabric showing between.

Appliquéd curtain with tabs

◀◀ see also ▶▶
Stitches p. 146
Borders and bindings p. 151

The last works of Matisse, made when he was all but bedridden in Saint Paul de Vence, have inspired many people. Certainly, Matisse's ideas are fun to play with; simply executed and without pretense, his images are much copied. The trick is to capture something of the spirit of the work, the sense of freedom and fun.

Applied pattern is designed to be seen, so make the curtain fullness just ten to twenty-five percent more than the fitting length. Tabbed headings can only be considered when the pole is low enough to reach the heading to draw the curtains. Wrap a length of spare fabric around the pole to calculate the tab length and width. The lining could be anything, but checks are easy to follow. This blue and white was chosen in the spirit of the whole, and is wrapped around to the

front, forming a simple border. To make the appliquéd pattern, which could be anything from a swarm of bees to a Gothic arch, find a simple rendering on the page of a book or gift card. Enlarge it onto squared paper or photocopy it to the size you want.

Preparation: Cut and join the curtain fabric. Cut out all appliqué pieces. Cut and join the lining, making it 6 cm (2½ in), or two whole checks bigger around than the curtain sides and hem. Cut a 12 cm (5 in) strip of lining fabric for the heading. Make up the tabs for the heading.

1 Set the appliqué pieces onto the curtain fabric. Pin the centers and across the raw edges, using as many pins as you can to keep the pieces flat during stitching. Stitch a wide satin stitch as tightly as possible, enclosing the raw edges completely, and making a raised border at the same time.

2 Trim away all threads and press thoroughly. Place the lining onto the table, press flat and pin or clamp to secure. Lie the stitched curtain over, matching the edges to the line of checks, or exactly 6 cm (2½ in) in. With small, light, stitches, herringbone the curtain to the lining.

3 Press the lining to the front. Fold under to make a hem and pin. Miter the corners. Slip stitch or ladder stitch the fabrics together along two sides and hem. Use small stitches so that you don't see any holes in the stitching.

4 Fold the tabs in half and position along the heading. Stitch securely. Pin the heading strip over, right sides and raw edges together. Match the checks at the ends. Stitch; press to the back and fold under. Slip stitch, catching into the stitched line.

It is important for the freshness of the design that both lining and appliqué are in the same color.

Patchwork curtains

◀◀ see also ▶▶
Folded ties p. 152   Pin-tucked curtain p. 76
Borders and bindings p. 151

Patchwork can be a random affair or be done to a carefully executed plan. It can be giant squares or jigsaw geometry; colors can be vibrant or mellow; fabrics may be specially selected or just remnants. A pile of disparate chintzes left over from a previous house provided inspiration for these curtains. As we cut and selected the pieces, no particular color theme emerged but a summer garden unfolded. Pattern is essential to good design and should relate to the scale of your windows.

Don't be too precious about matching colors; rather, try to include the whole spectrum and match the style of fabric. All of these are robust florals on the same weight of cloth.

Preparation: Plan the finished size of the curtain. Divide the width and drop into suitably sized squares. Add 1.5 cm (⅝ in) seam allowance to all sides of the finished square size. Add an additional amount for the border width, 3 cm (1¼ in), to all of the outer squares. Cut out, taking care to measure accurately to save matching problems later. Lay all the cut pieces out in order of appearance to check that you are happy with the result. Pin together in lengths and then number each length from the center of the window out.

Cut and make the ties. These are each 50 cm (20 in) in length and 3 cm (1¼ in) wide. Cut and join the border strips — you need to cut 24 cm (9½ in) for a 6 cm (2½ in) border.

1 Join the patchwork lengths together as pinned, with seams of 1.5 cm (⅝ in). Stitch the seams accurately, as each square also needs to meet its horizontal neighbour. Cut all the spare threads. Press the seams flat. Join the lengths to each other. Press the back and the front of the whole curtain thoroughly. If the fabric does pucker, try steaming with the hottest iron over a damp cloth. If you find that the seams just don't settle, interlining will help (use domette or sarille weight). Lay the lining over and pin the edges together. Trim so that they match exactly. Run a tacking thread all around, 4 cm (1½ in) from each edge.

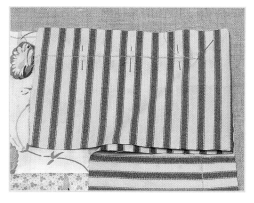

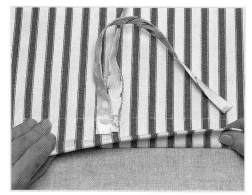

2 Pin the border all around, right sides and edges together. Start on the return side, about 2 cm (¾ in) from the hem or the heading, whichever will be least conspicuous. The stitching line will be just under 6 cm (2½ in) from the edge, so pin along and across this line. You might draw a pencil line to follow.

3 Fold the fabric sharply around the corner to make a triangular flap, which will miter in. Join the ends and stitch the border in place, along the pencilled line. At each corner, stitch right to the flap and secure, take the needle out, turn the curtain and insert the needle again on the opposite side of the flap, right next to the last stitch. Press from the front, miter the corners and fold the binding to the back, making a neat 6 cm (2½ in) border. Fold the corners under neatly, and fold the border in half again.

4 Pin the ties in pairs at even intervals along the border stitching line on the lining side and stitch securely. Fold the border in half to make a 6 cm (2½ in) border on the back of the curtain. Fold each corner flap under neatly, in the opposite direction to the one on the front. Slip stitch all around.

Headings with long ties are fun when there is enough space above the window for the curtain pole to be fixed at a suitable height.

The simplest ticking stripes are the perfect foil to country roses. Chintz teamed with stripes works because the colors harmonize.

Frills

Even those people and situations that seem at first sight to be above or beyond fashion can't fail to be affected eventually. Ten years ago, frilled edges were on every possible fabric in the home — curtains, sofa valances, cushions, valances — until there were frills on frills. Now, as with everything that becomes overdone, frilled edges are for the most part no longer in vogue. Of course, all this means is that they will soon be back in fashion again! And, in any case, many people, including myself, like frills. In the right place, that is.

Frills need to be handled carefully, and be used only when they are necessary to frame a window and lift a fabric. Never make frilled edges in fabric that contrasts strongly with the main fabric. Frills must settle in; it is not the color that's the focal point, it's the wavy edge. Frills are feminine, which is why they work best with soft colors and lightweight fabrics. Quite a bit of weight is added to the leading edge when a frill is stitched on, so all light fabrics will need to be lined if the edges are to be prevented from sagging.

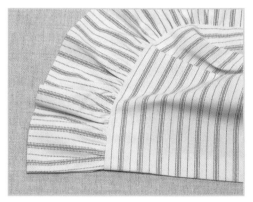

The simplest frills are single, stitched to the curtain on one side with a double hem at the other. Cut and join fabric two and half times the length to be frilled and 2.5 cm (1 in) wider than the finished frill. Press 1 cm (½ in) to the wrong side along the length and two short ends. Press under in half so the hem will be just under 0.5 cm (¼ in). Pin. Stitch close to the folded edge. Then run a gathering thread 1.5 cm (⅝ in) from the opposite side. Mark into four sections. Pull gathers up evenly within each of the four sections. Pin to the right side of the curtain. Stitch just outside the gathering stitches. Pull out the gathering threads. If the curtain is unlined, bind the raw edges. If lined, bring the lining to cover the stitching and slip stitch into the machine stitches.

Cut, join and make up the frill as above, but cut 2 cm (¾ in) wider than the finished frill and make 0.5 cm (¼ in) hems on both sides. Run two gathering threads very close together, approximately 3 cm (1¼ in) from one long edge. Mark the length into four sections and pull gathers up evenly within each. Press the curtain edge under 3 cm (1¼ in). Pin the gathers to this pressed line. Pin at least every 2 cm (¾ in), across the stitches. Stitch with a light satin stitch. Remove the gathering threads. At the back of the curtain, fold the 3 cm (1¼ in) turning in half to make a neat hem.

Cut and join fabric two and a half times the length to be frilled and twice the width of the finished frill, plus 4 cm (1½ in). Press in half lengthwise, right sides out. Fold the short ends under and stitch to close. Run two gathering threads very close together, 2 cm (¾ in) from the raw edges. Mark the length into four sections, and pull gathers up evenly within each. Pin to the curtain, matching the raw edges. Stitch close to the gathering line. Pull out the threads. Press the seam of the frill and curtain fabric to the back and herringbone stitch lightly to hold in place.

Above One of my favorite commissions was a delightful Queen Anne house which was decorated with such attention to detail that it always reminds me of a grown-up dolls' house. Every item has been positioned perfectly and every edging designed to the last detail.

Left The frilled edges here serve only to soften the frame to the view beyond. Nothing in the soft tones of either fabric or binding arrests the eye, but they create a sense of quiet sophistication.

Interlined Curtains

Thick, interlined curtains look completely wonderful if they are made in the simplest way, with no decoration or complicated processes. There are four main reasons to interline curtains: to improve the drape of a fine fabric; to absorb annoying sound; to catch the weather's worst; and to make a room as dark as possible. If you need and want thick curtains, they might as well be long and luxurious, falling in generous folds. Just choose an interesting but uncomplicated fabric, and if you want to jazz it up, add some breathtaking tiebacks or stitch cords and fringes onto the finished curtain.

Noise

Double-glazed windowpanes eliminate most out-side sound, which is fine when windows are closed, but not if you prefer to leave them open. How you deal with this will largely depend on your window and location. You could fit a heavy shade close to the glass, but there isn't always the room and many windows are unsuitable — for instance, if shutters close across inside or if light is at a premium.

Heavy fabrics absorb sound extremely efficient-ly and with a substantial interlining you can create an effective sound barrier. If you have a problem with either general or specific noise, the thicker and heavier you make your curtains the better. Curtains might not help you in the day, but can improve life in the evenings and early mornings when you are trying to sleep, relax or socialize. If you need to sleep in the daytime and like to have air flowing through open windows, the thickest, darkest curtains possible can be lifesavers. Although thick curtains are often chosen to pre-vent drafts completely, an open window behind drawn curtains will provide enough gentle move-ment for air to filter through in a refreshing, rather than an intrusive, way.

Above A wonderfully soft, cream damask is finished with elaborately draped, hand-woven cords and tassels. The pole, rings and finials are antique white, finished with gold leaf.

Left Block checks in a subtle combination of blue-green and off-white are lively, light and airy for a country view. Heavy interlining gives body and weight to the fine taffeta, and provides draft proofing. Hand-gathered headings keep the overall window design informal.

Light

Most people want the option to filter the light and at other times to cut it out completely. You may not want both in the same room, but it is worth considering having sheer and heavy curtains together at bedroom windows. While you are geared up to make one pair of curtains, you might make two, even if you only use butter muslin, which costs less than a couple of pounds a meter. Other fabrics suitable for lightweight curtains that will fold up easily behind heavier ones are linen or cotton voile, calico, silk habutai, taffeta, synthetic silk, broderie anglaise, spot muslin, jute scrim, and any lacework or open weave fabric.

The thickest curtains are perfect for insomniacs; with a dense lining it is possible to completely black out any light. When we have a serious request for complete blackness, we prefer to lock in an extra liner of dense black cotton between the interlining and the curtain lining.

Above Double-layer silk curtains are tied back to allow maximum light onto an imposing staircase. Light from a higher landing shines onto the curtains, reflecting the cinnamon, ginger and red ochre tones in the folds.

Above right Creamy wool and cotton crewelwork curtains frame the window, pulling right back to allow the light to bounce off the deep window recesses.

Right Heavy chenille fabrics are weighty enough to prevent most drafts. Fringing the sides in sympathetic tones softens the edges.

Left A sympathetic check is often the perfect companion to a printed chintz.

Interlining fabrics

Interlinings are usually at least ninety percent cotton and brushed so that the raised fibers will hold the heat. The heaviest, known as 'bump', can be as thick as a good army blanket, and you can actually use old blankets. The finest is as light as a warm shawl — again, if you have a decent length of natural material in the cupboard, such as brushed cotton sheets, you could use these. Domette is the finest of the interlinings. In general, it is best to choose an interlining similar in weight to the curtain fabric, but you can also use a thick one to bulk out a silk or a fine one to soften the drape of dense wool. It is vital not to cheat on the locking-in process, especially if the fabrics don't immediately cling to each other. And if you are fixing a fine top fabric to a heavy liner, you should double the amount of locking. It is sometimes a good idea to test the different effects. Make up a couple of short lengths of fabric with a couple of interlinings and pin them against the window.

We do also use a synthetic interlining called sarille. It's not as heavy as cotton and it is inclined to 'walk' over time. It doesn't give quite the bulk of cotton twill, but being lighter it is much easier to work with. Certainly, if you are a beginner and need to make large curtains, I strongly suggest you start with sarille. We find it most useful in potentially 'wet' areas, such as kitchens and bathrooms, because it dry cleans more easily than cotton and won't pick up a damp smell.

Top fabrics

However heavy the curtain fabric, I still prefer to stitch it to an interlining; thick curtains need to look and feel luxurious. The interlining doesn't even have to be thick, heavy bump; the lightest domette will greatly improve the drape and fall. I can't think that there is any technical restriction to your choice of fabric, so the usual criteria of location, view and budget are really the deciding factors.

Above Rich red and gold silks draped onto the floor add a little welcome opulence to a country dining and music room. Low ceilings and small windows ask for simplicity, which has not been compromised.

Left Coral silk curtains complement the extraordinarily beautiful valance. A find at an antiques fair, its handwork is intricate, fine and well preserved and needs no competition.

Left and below Lightweight under curtains are used most frequently here, while the heavily interlined outer curtains are pulled right across for dark cold evenings. Soft colors and light fabrics always look less bulky than deeper colored, heavier fabrics, even when the curtains drape onto the floor.

Above If it's inconvenient to fit a door between dressing room or bathroom and bedroom, a curtain can be draped back to soften the transition, or dropped down to cover fully.

Left Sheer under curtains in light, open weave linen filter the early morning sun gently, but there is still the option, on a miserable day, to pull the heavy curtains and close the world out. The taupe inset strips pick up the soft browns in the delicate rose print.

Making interlinings

◀◀ see also ▶▶

Making curtain interlinings p. 17   Mitered corners p. 145
Estimating for curtain fabric p. 19   Stitches p.146

Preparation: Cut required lengths of fabric, interlining and lining and join as necessary with flat seams. Place the fabric face down onto your worktable. Line up the leading edge along one long side and the hem to one short side of the table. The curtain is most likely to be wider than the table, so leave the rest dropping over the side. Sweep your meter or yard rule over the fabric to smooth out every crease; clamp or pin it to the table. Press. Place the interlining on top, lining up seams, sides and hems. Smooth out.

1 Lock stitch the interlining to the main fabric along the length on each seam and half way between. Do so every 35 cm (14 in) if joining a fine fabric to heavy interlining. Don't skimp on this job or your curtains will look a mess in a couple of months. Fold the interlining back on itself at the first seam and stitch all the way down, using double thread. Stop about 20 cm (8 in) short of the hem and the top. Fold the interlining back flat, smooth out and then fold back again at the next stitching line.

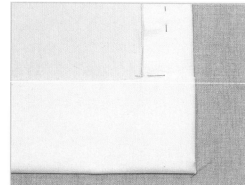

2 Trim the interlining sides and hem flush with the main fabric. Remove the clamps or pins and fold over both fabric and interlining 8 cm (3¼ in). Make sure the interlining is well tucked into the fold and a solid, firm edge is pinned in place. Fold the hem up by 12 cm (4¾ in).

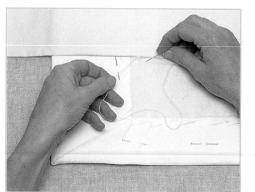

6 Lay the lining over the interlining, matching up the seam lines and allowing the lining to overhang the hem by approximately 10 cm (4 in). Smooth out and lock the lining to the interlining along the length as before.

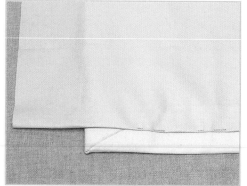

7 Score the lining along the folded edge of the curtain. Trim to this line. Fold the raw edge under 3 cm (1¼ in) and pin the length of the curtain, leaving 3 cm (1¼ in) of the curtain fabric showing.

8 Trim the lining hem to 8 cm (4 in) from the curtain hem. Pin this edge to the hem fold. Take up the excess fabric by finger-pressing a pleat into the lining along the stitched hemline. Press the fold downwards and pin to hold in place.

3 Press the hem in place lightly and pin. Miter the bottom corner with a long miter. If you are using the heaviest interlining, cut the bulk away following the fold lines. (If you ever need to lengthen the curtains you'll just have to sew a patch.)

4 Stitch the side of the curtain using long stitch. Catch both layers of interlining, but not the face fabric. If you are using penny weights, insert one into the corner and stitch to the back of the hem fold. If you prefer to use chain weight, secure at the corner and then catch stitch all the way along.

5 Pin the hem back up and close the miter with ladder stitch. Stitch the hem with herringbone stitch. When you reach the end of the table, lift the curtain carefully and move over so that you can work on the other half, or at least the next section.

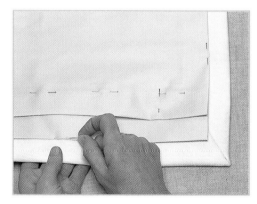

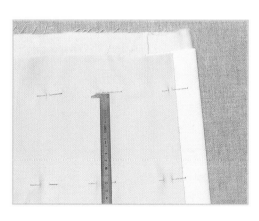

9 Fold the raw edge of the lining under 3 cm (1¼ in) to match the sides. Pin.

10 Measure from hem to mark hook drop. Pin through all three layers to hold all fabrics together securely. Measure and pin all the way across at 30 cm (12 in) intervals. Slip stitch the lining in place, stopping at hook drop. Move the curtain across the table and finish first side in the same way. Turn the curtain so that the heading is at the long side of the table

and work on the whole width at one go. Check the exact overall drop measurement and mark with a row of pins into the lining only. Fold the lining back on itself and trim the interlining along the pinned line. Pin and then herringbone the interlining to the curtain fabric. Fold the lining back, pin to the curtain fabric and make your chosen heading.

Hand-pleated headings

Pleated headings are best suited to formal situations — anywhere the curtains need to fold back neatly and tidily. If you want the headings to stand up above the fitting, to reach the ceiling of a room or recess, make a fabric covered lath. If you want to see a decorative pole, then headings are neater hanging beneath. Use under a valance when the curtaining is formal or when you need to stack the curtains back into limited space.

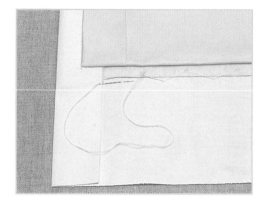

Preparation: Adjust the depth of the pleats according to the length of the curtains. As a rule of thumb, use 10 cm (4 in) buckram for curtains up to 2.5 meters (2¾ yards) and 13.5 cm (5¼ in) up to 3 meters (3¼ yards) and 15 cm (6 in) for any greater length. For short, sill-length curtains, cut the buckram down to 7 or 8 cm (2¾ or 3¼ in).

1 Mark the overall drop at the top and fold the lining back onto itself. Trim the interlining away and herringbone to the curtain fabric. Measure just under double the depth of the buckram and trim away any excess fabric evenly.

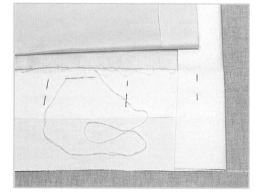

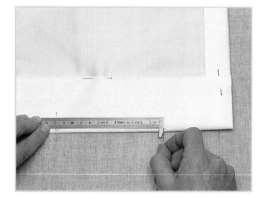

2 Place the buckram on the fabric against the cut edge of the interlining and stitch to hold. You can just catch the buckram to the interlining a few times across the width on short curtains.

3 Bring the lining over and trim to match the fabric. Fold both over the buckram so that the raw edges go right up inside the heading. Pin and press. Slip stitch the ends to close.

4 Check that the finished width of the curtain is as expected and pin to mark the pleats, gap overlaps and return allowances in place. Fold pleats and pin firmly in position at the top and bottom of the buckram. (Inverted pleats are stitched towards the back.) Machine down the length, fastening threads securely. Remove pins, turn to front and pleat up.

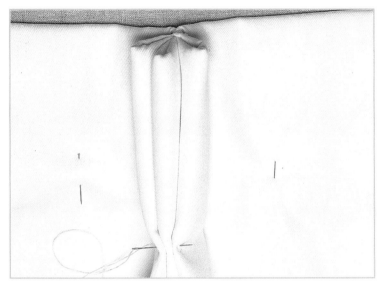

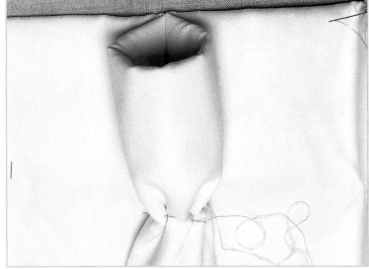

French pleats

Open out the pleat, place two or three fingers inside and flatten. Lift the pleat, pinch in the center fold, then push down to make three equal pleats. Pin together at the base and stitch through all three pleats. At the top of the pleat, stitch each in position to hold its shape and then stitch through all three to push the pleat forwards.

Goblet pleats

Open out the pleat and run a gathering thread around the base just below the buckram, using double or buttonhole thread. Pull up tightly and secure. Roll a rectangle of interlining 2 cm (¾ in) shorter than the buckram and thick enough to fill the pleat. Cut a separate piece for each pleat, and stuff it well into each goblet to bulk out.

Double pleats

Open out the pleat, place a couple of fingers inside and flatten. Press both sides to the center to make two equal pleats. Pin together at the base. At the top of the pleat, stitch through each pleat and through both to push them forwards. Take the pin out of the base and stitch through the center just to hold lightly. Press lightly.

Inverted pleats

Work from the back of the curtain. Open out the pleat, place a couple of fingers inside and flatten. Pin flat and press lightly. Secure the flat pleat to the top of the curtain. At the bottom, stitch to the end of the stitching line and catch the edges down. Stitch through interlining and lining without pulling on the front of the curtain fabric.

Gathered headings

Use where there are uneven tops to windows or ceilings that need to be disguised and in any informal situation. This might be in a country house or in a relaxed room in a more formal house. Gathered, or frilled, headings soften the overall finish. Usually the curtains should also be just bumping or softly draping onto the floor so that the whole look is casual. You won't be able to pull gathered headings away from the window, as they will take up more room than, say, a formal pleated top. Either use tiebacks to drape the curtains back or twist the lining around to hold the curtains away from the window.

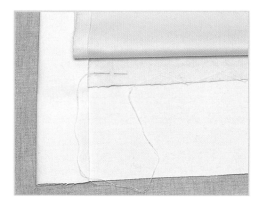
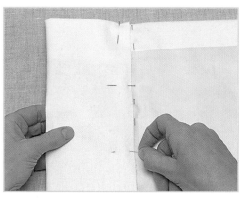

1 Measure the overall drop. Fold the lining back along the marked line; trim the interlining to this line. Herringbone stitch the interlining to the curtain fabric.

2 Smooth the lining back down, measure the distance you have planned for the heading frill and the gathering from the interlining. For instance, if you have planned a 10 cm (4 in) frill with 4 cm (1½ in) of gathering stitches, mark

14 cm (5½ in) from the overall drop. Trim both fabrics along this line, fold over and press to the lining side. Machine or hand stitch as planned. Gather up and stitch hook band to cover all workings.

Deeply gathered headings offer an informal, soft finish, partly hiding the pole and fittings.

If it is greater than 8–10 cm (3¼-4 in), the frill will start to flop over in places, and will need stiffening to stand higher.

Hook band

You may not want to spend the extra time to do this, but if you want a professional finish, a fabric hook band is the best, to make your curtains as good inside as out. Made from either the curtain or lining fabric, this band secures the curtain hooks, covers all gathering stitches and holds each pleat in place.

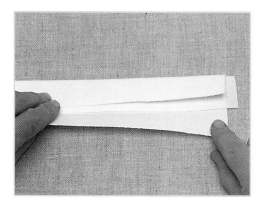  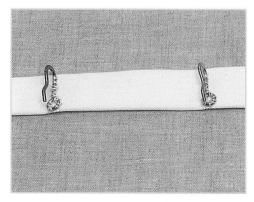

1 Cut a strip of buckram or heading tape the width of the gathers and the pull up length. Cut fabric the same length, plus 4 cm (1½ in) and three times as wide. Press the fabric around the stiffening.

2 Fold the raw ends under, trimming away any excess layers. Trim 0.5 cm (¼ in) from the long edge and herringbone stitch along the length.

3 Divide the hook band into as many equal sections as you need. Stitch the hooks in position securely. The hooks look neater stitched onto the back, with only the drop of the hooks showing at the front, but are easier stitched neatly to the front.

When you want the frill to flop over, make it at least 12 cm (4¾ in) and up to 15 cm (6 in) deep and don't add any extra stiffening.

A hook band stitched behind holds the gathers straight and helps the frilled heading to draw back in soft folds.

Hand-gathered headings

Although the full method is below, you can cheat here and use bought tape. Hand stitch it to the curtain using running stitches and pull up using the given cords. Cover with a hook band, stitching the gathers evenly across the width. If you decide to use a double frill here, allow the frill return on the lining piece as well. Fold both back and then make up as one.

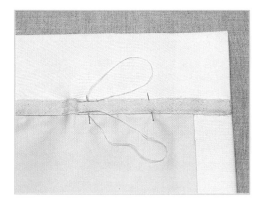

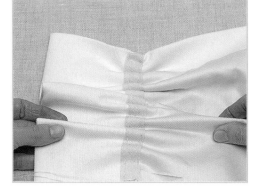

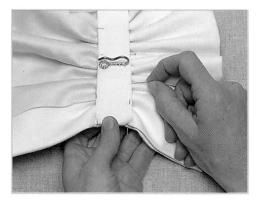

1 Divide the whole width into ten equal sections. Subdivide if the curtain is more than two and a half widths wide. Mark each division with a colored tack. Pin flat heading tape to just cover the raw edge. Work with two long needles and double or buttonhole thread. Make two rows of stitches, one close to the bottom of the tape and one close to the top. Use a small gauge to keep the rows parallel and the stitches even.

2 Work between the markers — you can probably do half a width at each time, depending on the thickness of the curtain. Pull up each section to a tenth of the required width, or to correspond to your subdivision. Finger-press the gathers evenly and tie off the threads so that there is no visible gap between sections.

3 Pin and stitch the hook band (see method as described on page 113) over the heading tape.

Cotton checks are ideal for children's rooms, giving color without being too dominant. If you are using a geometric pattern, position all of your headings and hems so that all folds and stitching lines are running with the given lines.

The lining and curtain can be separated at the heading to make a double frill. Fold the front layer towards the back and the lining towards the front. Gather the headings together as one and stitch the hooks and hook band on the inner side.

Before you even cut a checked or striped fabric, make sure that the weave or print is 'on grain'. Showing this perfect example illustrates how awful the headings would look if the checks were distorted and uneven.

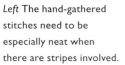

Above The lovely ice-cream colors seem to reflect the outside at every time of day — the golds pick up the morning sun, the hot pinks glow in the middle of the day and the mauves and blues echo the sky at twilight.

Left The hand-gathered stitches need to be especially neat when there are stripes involved.

Rolled edge and bunched headings

This way of making a rolled edge and hem is the easiest I have found and doesn't take long to do. You need to choose a good cord to stitch to the inner edge of the roll. Whether you have a discreet self-colored cord or an indiscreet highly colored contrast, the extra texture 'identifies' the border and covers the stitching line. The rolls are made from interlining, so you will need an extra length.

Preparation: The rolls are made from interlining. Cut a length of interlining for each leading edge and each hem, 30 cm (12 in) wide if the interlining is heavy and wider if not. There should be no joins, or the neat, smooth roll won't be!

These curtains are quite theatrical, with their frilled heading and rolled edges. You can arrange the folds as you think fit — the stiffer the roll, the more dramatic the curves.

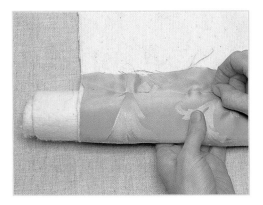

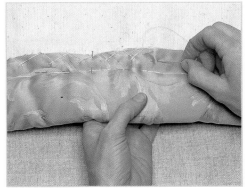

1 Following the general instructions on pages 108 and 109, lock the interlining to the main fabric (see Preparation) and the lining to the interlining (step 6). Don't miter the corners or make the hem. Fold the lining back out of the way. Place the roll 8 cm (3¼ in) in from the edge. Fold the curtain front over and pin tight against the roll. There should be 2–3 cm (¾–1¼ in) of curtain fabric still beyond the roll. If not, make the fold bigger.

2 Stitch the roll in place with long stitch or long running stitches, secured every so often with back stitches. Miter the bottom corners, making sure that the rolls are jammed tight together to make a solid corner. You might need to herringbone the raw edges down if the fabric is springy.

3 Bring the lining over and slip stitch neatly against the roll. If you want to use a contrast lining, pipe it first to give yourself a good edge to stitch against. Stitch cord to the right side of the finished curtain. Make sure you cover the stitching line, and use a gauge to check the distance of the cord from the edge.

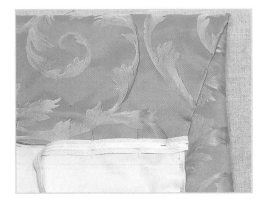

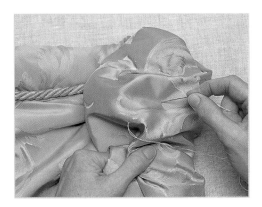

4 To make the bunched heading, trim the roll at the overall drop measurement and leave the interlining in (see p. 109, step 10) as the extra bulk will help. Fold heading over and make gathers as on page 114. It's fine to use bought tape, as the bunches and scrunches cover it completely. But you do need a hook band (see p. 113), as the pleats need to be evenly spaced and the back of the tape sometimes becomes visible, as the headings drop a bit over time.

5 Pull the heading frill up into both hands and scrunch it up until you like the shape. Using a long needle and strong thread, stitch through randomly, sometimes through to the back of the curtain and sometimes just weaving in and out of the folds. Use as few threads as possible — but too few mean that the heading won't hold its shape.

Italian stringing

◀◀ see also ▶▶
Bought trimmings p. 150
Headings p. 86
Curtain poles p. 25

I have no idea at all why this style is referred to as Italian stringing. It is sometimes called 'reefed'. Theater curtains are operated in the same manner — just a system of rings and cords that take the fabric upward rather than across the opening.

We usually design reefed curtains as a solution to a specific problem. After all, any curtain can be fixed at the top and tied back. Reefed curtains don't need tiebacks, so there is a great simplicity in the look of the curtain drawn back. While you might leave reefed curtains untouched for most of the time, there is always the option to raise and lower them as much as you wish. Choose this style if there is an ugly view to hide, as it is then essential that light be introduced to the room at low level. They are also suitable for a modern, minimal room where fuss needs to be eliminated; for a situation where the fabric is an important component; when you can't

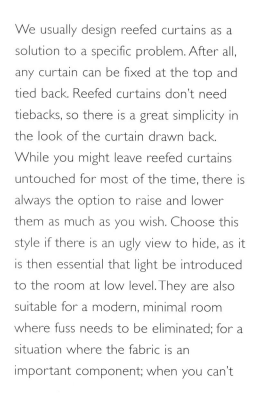

Windows that encroach on a roof or attic space always cause curtain problems. Wherever there is enough light, fixed curtains that draw back and can be dropped down easily are my preferred option for both form and function.

reach a tieback because the window is set high; and when you want curtains to stay put without any bother.

Any heading at all can be chosen — tabbed; goblet, triple or inverted pleats; gathered; smocked; eyelets; ruched onto a pole or flat. Or anything else your imagination can conjure up. And any fitting is usable, such as a very simple pole, a track and lath, an elaborate pole, an under valance fitting or simply a self-colored batten.

To create these curtains, the fittings need to be in place and the curtains finished. Hang the curtains and fit so that the headings join together at the top. Take a long piece of string and tie one curtain back to the position you want as if it were a tieback. Pin or nail the string into the wall to hold in place. This is where you will fix the cord carrier.

Stand on a ladder and finger-fold one of the curtains into pleats until you like the shape of the drape. Mark the front and back of each fold with a pin or tailor's tack, following the line of the string. Take the curtains down and lie the marked one onto the worktable, front down. Stitch a small brass ring to each of the marks representing the back of a fold. (If you don't want to see the rings, cover the whole circle with button-hole stitches in matching thread.) Tie and

Italian stringed or reefed curtains are raised and lowered by cords stitched at the back of the curtains, leaving the headings in the same place. Elaborate cording, once fixed, remains undisturbed.

stitch one end of cord to the ring nearest the leading edge. Thread through each ring and leave the end dangling.

Hang the curtains back up. Thread the cord through the carrier fixed to the wall. Knot the end neatly, or attach a key tassel instead. Fit a cleat lower down on the wall so that you are sure to reach the cords comfortably.

Contrast linings

Where a curtain will be seen from both sides, the lining needs to be considered as carefully as the main fabric. Color is obviously important, but so are durability and texture. If you want the curtain to look as though it has two good sides, the back or lining should be of equal weight and quality. This might mean that you choose the same fabric for both sides or that you pick complementary textiles, of the same weave and construction but plain one side and pattern on the other. And by the way, if you don't make the best job of stitching the front and back fabrics together along the edge, cover them with a chunky cord and no one will be any the wiser.

Fabrics

There's no shortage of choice of fabrics, but you probably won't want to spend too much on the linings. Striped cotton ticking is, perhaps uniquely, both inexpensive and smart, and it comes in good colors. We use miles of ticking in terra cotta, taupe,

Above Contrast linings don't have to be obvious to be effective. Here a deeper colored lining that harmonizes with the curtain color subtly adds another dimension and depth to the whole.

Far left In a corridor, room dividers or door curtains of the same fabric might be used on both sides. Take care to match pattern or stripe exactly; if the fabric pattern makes this difficult, stitch a cord along the edge to cover the join.

Left The striking lining is a statement, making clear that two separate rooms are involved.

Above **Children love to play inside long curtains, and the lining used here is just for fun. As they grow, the lining can be changed, leaving the checked fronts for another scheme.**

Right **Instead of a cupboard door, a flat curtain covers hanging clothes. The striped lining is fun, and it is as easy to make a curtain of this size with a lining as without. If you feel adventurous, you could stitch sock pockets to the inside.**

denim blue, cinnamon and ochre, as well as olive green and black. Basic, old-fashioned gingham checks look great and fit all budgets. You can use the same fabric back and front, particularly for hallways, doors and room or corridor dividers.

Have a look from outside the house to make sure the lining doesn't scream at you. Strong colors are almost always taboo, as they look ghastly from outside; so keep to soft tones, unless you live in an isolated position and something daring looks absolutely right.

Choose complementary linings as a design element. A pretty lining seen as you sit in a window seat is a joy and is welcoming behind a door curtain. A strong print can make an interesting statement in an otherwise plain room. Children like to hide behind curtains, and never pull them properly, so you might as well pay as much attention to the inner as the outer fabric. Something washable is always a good idea.

Where the lining will be on show permanently and is therefore as important as the front fabric, stitch the two together along the edge. Linings that play a minor role, designed to be seen for fun or to provide a sliver of interest when the curtains are twisted back, may be stitched back as you would a plain lining, or along the edges.

Door curtains *(Left, above)*

When making door curtains or room dividers, where each side is as important as the other, the lining should be brought right to the edge. Make the curtain in exactly the same way, but cut the lining 5 cm (2 in) bigger than the finished curtain. Fold the lining under exactly along the folded curtain edge. Stitch the fabrics together with a short ladder stitch. Checks are especially tricky to match, so avoid them if you don't want the bother.

Piped edge *(Left, below)*

Piping can be stitched either to the curtain fabric or to the lining. If you want it on the front, it is best to stitch the piping to the fabric before you interline. You will need to lock stitch the interlining along the piping stitching line and herringbone the piped edge down securely. Then slip stitch the lining right into the machine stitching line.

Piped lining *(Facing page, left, above)*

If you want to set the lining to show a border of the main fabric at the back, a piped edge on the lining looks neat. Cut the lining 2-3 cm (¾–1¼ in) smaller than the finished curtain. Stitch the piping around and press the raw edges under. Place onto your curtain and lock in. Stitch through the back of the piping into the curtain with small, neat, running stitches.

Rope *(Facing page, left, below)*

The only thing you have to remember with rope or cord is to keep it straight. If you let it fall around your feet as you put it on, the twist will show when the curtain is hanging. Seriously twisted, chunky cord can pull the edge out of shape. So to keep the cord even and straight, unwind it all from the card and pin it to the fabric before you start. Make sure you don't pull or push it as you stitch; catch it to the fabric with stitches 1.5–2 cm (⅝–¾ in) long and use double or buttonhole thread.

Choose your linings carefully for each situation. Most of these have been devised to add some drama and will be very visible from outside. The toile de Jouy lining of the landing curtains (above and left) is in fact the more important of the two fabrics. It is used in this way because the curtains are never dropped.

Mixing and matching fabrics

You may see the perfect fabric, but can't work it into the budget, or perhaps you just can't find what you want. On the other hand, you may feel that a plain fabric is just too much of a single color, that stripes are not suitable and that you can't find a print or weave of perfect scale and coloring. It's not such a bad idea then to work with several fabrics, cutting and joining as necessary to make exactly what you want. Just make sure the fabrics are of the same consistency and construction, so that they don't pull against each other.

Stripes

You might want green and red, but not as a pattern, so try cutting two, three or more lengths into five or six different width strips and stitching them together randomly. It really doesn't matter if the leading edges and returns match each other or not.

The gold panels are stitched into dark coral/terra cotta curtains like slips of light. The rich suffused reds of walls and curtains blend together at night, lifted by the lights of gold.

Wallpaper and curtains in similar tones are kind and restful for a sleeping area. The creamy whites and aqua blues frame the view to open countryside beyond, or close over to become one with the delicate toile de Jouy walls.

One of the most difficult situations for which to choose a fabric is one where the drawn over curtains will become the wall. You probably won't want to match the wall; a geometric or floral design can become tiring; and a plain color may be boring or overpowering. Here we solved the problem by joining three different but complementary colors in random strips. Hand-pleated headings encourage the curtains to fall in soft folds.

In fact, it is probably better that they don't, as then at least the curtains will be truly individual; it's the overall effect that matters.

Insets

It often happens that a single color is just too powerful or too solid for the room. You still want to use the chosen color, but need a bit of light relief. Draw onto squared paper and design your own combination of stripes, borders and squares. Always bear in mind the size and proportions of your windows and balance the shapes accordingly.

Colors

Consider which color, if any, that you want to be predominant. A livelier, brighter color might be set alongside a heavier, denser color to give flashes of light, or two deep colors, such as burgundy and purple, can be used together to give close, resonant hues of the same tone. Two colors from the same spectrum, such as pink and red, can be combined with vibrant, exciting results. For a contemporary room, splashes of silver, copper or gold can be used to lift almost any color. Light and dark can be played against each other to relieve and complement — white with black, oyster and gray, taupe and soft terra cotta, to suggest just a few.

A border for an interlined curtain

◀◀ see also ▶▶
Borders and bindings p. 151
Ties p. 152

You can follow these instructions to make a border around the edge of any interlined curtains. For very heavy fabric and long curtains, always choose a border rather than a binding, so that the fabric lies flat at the back of the curtain.

For small curtains, keep the border narrow and always use fabric of similar weight to the main material. For a small curtain without much bulk, lock the interlining to the main fabric before you begin, tack together approximately 1.25 cm (about ½ in) in from the raw edges and trim straight if necessary. Make these two layers up as one and leave out step 3 below.

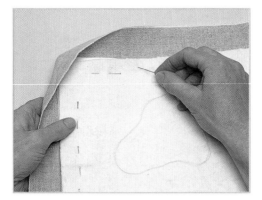

3 Press the border strip away from the curtain. Turn over and lay the interlining over. Lock in the usual way. Trim the edges exactly to the curtain fabric. Tack together just 1.5 cm (⅝ in) from the edges.

Preparation: Make the border at least 2 cm (¾ in) finished width to take up the extra bulk of interlining; but not more than 10 cm (4 in), as you will find it difficult to keep the fabrics flat. The border strips should be cut three times the width of the finished border, plus 2–5 cm (¾–2 in) to fall behind the lining. A cotton chintz or poplin will be fine with 2 cm (¾ in)

extra, but a heavy weave or velvet will need the 5 cm (2 in).

For the small curtain here, a border 2 cm (¾ in) wide is enough. Cut strips of fabric 8 cm (3 in) for three sides of each curtain. For the heading, cut strips 9 cm (3½ in) wide. Join all strips on the cross to minimize the effect of the seam and to keep the bulk of it to a minimum.

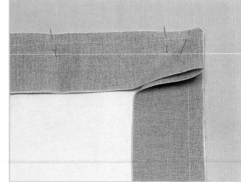

4 Fold the border to the back, making a neat edge 2 cm (¾ in) wide. Miter the corners neatly at the front. Press and pin.

1 Place the curtain onto your worktable right side up, lining up the leading edge with one long side and the hem with one short side. Start at the heading and pin the binding to the curtain along the length, right sides together. Work down to the first corner and stop just under 2 cm (¾ in) from the edge. Fold the binding over at a right angle to make a triangular flap, pin along the diagonal to hold in place and continue pinning three sides and two corners.

2 Stitch the binding to the fabric, just under 2 cm (¾ in) from the raw edge. Stop at each corner flap and secure your stitch. Take the needle out, turn the curtain, fold the flap over. Put the needle back in exactly next to the last stitch to make a neat corner. Work round three sides.

5 Miter each corner at the back neatly, folding the triangular flaps in the opposite direction to the one on the front. Herringbone stitch to the interlining along the three sides.

Right Knotted ties in the lining fabric soften the strong print of the main curtains.

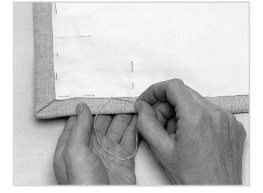

Above Bold patterns can be the best solution for rooms and windows that have strength of character.

6 Lay the lining over the curtain and lock in. Score the lining along the edge of the border. Trim along this line. Press under 2 cm (¾ in) so that the binding looks the same back and front, and pin. Keep the three layers together at the top with pins. Slip stitch three sides.

7 To make the heading, pin and stitch the heading binding to the front. Press to the back, leaving the same 1.25 cm (about ½ in) of binding showing. Pin. Fold the sides under neatly and slip stitch.

8 Fold the binding in half, press and slip stitch. Stitch inverted pleats at approximately 12–15 cm (4¾–6 in) intervals. Stitch two ties – each 28 cm (about 12 in) long – to the back of each pleat.

Quilting

As with so many crafts that we now consider decorative, quilting started as an absolutely practical solution for a severe domestic need. Sheep's wool stuffed between two layers of fabric made the perfect early insulation for outdoor clothing. Stitching the outer covers together held the wool in place, and this we now call quilting. True to the creative nature of man, more and more elaborate designs and patterns have been invented and worked, to the point that quilting has become an art form. The best-preserved antique bed quilts fetch a premium in the salerooms.

I am not suggesting anything on the art or museum scale here, but if you want to add depth, richness, and originality to a plain fabric — nothing can hold a candle to quilting. Quilted fabrics are tactile, they feel nice and sumptuous — few people can resist putting out their hands to touch a comforting quilted fabric. And the insulating properties of a quilted fabric should be considered, especially for door curtains. Of course, hand quilting is time-consuming, but then so are most things worth bothering with. Think of the consistent, even stitching as therapeutic and save it for a winter weekend or long evenings in front of the fire.

Fabric

Any natural fiber — cotton, wool, silk or linen — is fine for quilting. Felted wools, old linen sheets, shot taffeta and even towelling can be quilted. The smoother the weave the more prominent the quilted effect. A heavy fabric is more difficult to move around, so either choose quilting for a small curtain or work on the worktable.

Design

There are many good books dedicated to quilting and quilting patterns. Choose for your capability and for the style of the room. An intricate floral and scallop design that would look stunning in a country bedroom could be a disaster in a contemporary hallway. Oversized checks could be quite brilliant for either, but draw to scale on an old sheet first to see what you would be getting.

We devised this swinging pole to hold the curtains in order that the shutters might still be used, and the woodwork remains visible as much as possible.

Left and inset Quilting stitched through to both sides is the perfect way to decorate double-sided curtains where the fabric itself is unpatterned.

Quilted border curtains

It is relatively simple to quilt a border that is then stitched to the hem and leading edge of thick curtains. The extra weight and definition offers interesting detail to these curtains, without being in any way obtrusive.

Below Shades and curtains cover different windows in the same room. The quilted hem adds weight to the long door curtains, which hang in heavy folds.

Inset The same fabric has been used for the subtle detailing of quilting and border, but this could be an opportunity to introduce new color or pattern.

Cut strips of curtain fabric and interlining to fit either the length of the hem and leading edge or the hem only. The width doesn't really matter much, but say approximately 20–25 cm (8–10 in) for average room height. Cut and make up enough piping to go along both sides of the border.

Pin and tack the fabric and interlining together and plan your quilting pattern.

◀◀ see also ▶▶
Roman shades p. 40
Making interlinings p. 108
Hand-pleated headings p. 110
Piping p. 153

Diamonds or squares are effective and simple to do. Mark the stitching lines with colored tacks or tailor's chalk. Stitch with machined or hand stitches. Always start from the same side or the fabrics will walk and you will just get ugly creasing. Stitch the piping to both long sides approx. 1.5 cm (⅝ in) from either side. Press raw edges under and herring-bone to the interlining at the back.

Place the border along the leading edge and hem of the curtain, 6 cm (2½ in) from the outside edges. Miter the corner. Pin, press and sew to the fabric with running stitches, pushing the needle through close to the piping. Make up the curtain as on page 108-9, folding hem and leading side in 6 cm (2½ in) along piped edge. Bring lining right up to the quilted border and slip stitch to piping.

Right The quilted border here has been stitched to the leading edge and to the hem to give a weight and gravitas that underline the function of this library function room.

Below The narrow piped edge is a useful but barely noticeable definition to both sides of the border. It can be easier to stitch to a piped line than to one that is just pressed under.

Valances

Valances go in and out of fashion, yet in some ways they are beyond the very idea of fashion. In certain circumstances and with particular styles of decorating, valances are always the correct design solution and they have endured over years of changing tastes.

The problem has been that when valances are considered to be in fashion they have tended to be overstyled, decorated to an excess that means that everyone goes off them again for a while. Then they are pronounced unfashionable until the whole thing comes round again. But if you choose the correct style of valance for the room and the overall design of the furnishings in the house, it can provide the perfect finish to a window treatment.

Style and proportion

Smart houses need smart decoration and design, while comfortable, rough round the edges sorts of houses need less formal furnishings — and minimalist homes need everything absolutely perfect. The valance you want to make now might be the essence of simplicity — no more than a frill inside a cottage window — or it might be a huge corded and tasselled affair destined for an important period window.

Broadly speaking, valances fall into two categories — gathered and flat — and most styles are variations on one or other of these basic methods. Gathered valances can be made with any of the heading styles used for curtains, whereas flat valances are restricted to applied designs, such as cords. The hems of both can be either straight or shaped to almost any design.

The rule of thumb for the depth of a valance is one fifth of the overall drop of the curtains or of the floor to ceiling measurement. It is usual to start a valance just below the cornice and to finish just below the top of the window recess. Fit right to the ceiling if a room is less than two and a half meters (eight feet) high, but if the window is set very low, fabric to the ceiling might look ridiculous, so make a judgment about the positioning by eye. Make sure that tall, ugly fittings at the top of the recess are fully covered; you don't want air vents, roller shade fittings and so on destroying the line.

Elaborate pole drapes and swags and tails are a different consideration altogether. They are usually best left to the professionals, as the proportions and draping are complex and must be excellent in order to look right. Only make drapery if you have a suitable, tall Georgian or Victorian window, and then only try it if you are a very competent and patient needleworker.

Fabrics are usually chosen to match the curtains, but there is no real reason why they should be. If your curtains are plain, elaborately woven damask could be a luxurious complement or you might put a plain color, cottage style, over a block check, or vice versa. Fabrics that attract dust aren't a good idea, and don't try to gather too large patterns, or you could spoil the whole effect.

Timeless fabrics and styles, such as country bedrooms in toile de Jouy, small floral prints and rustic stripes, ask for soft valances to frame the window. Here simplicity is all and the homemade look is much more attractive than overly perfect work or something too formal.

Design and making

Gathered valances are really just small curtains. The interlining and/or lining are locked together in the same way; bindings, borders and headings are also made in exactly the same way. You don't have the corners to worry about, as the valance is long and thin instead of big and bulky.

Linings and interlinings are made up in the same way as the curtain, so, for example, an interlined valance goes over interlined curtains. For a valance, I often use interlining that is a degree lighter than that used for the curtains. This is because valances that are gathered or folded can become quite bulky, and because they are short they can stick out like small skirts if they are too chunky. You want the linings to look the same from outside, so choose the same lining for the valance as the curtains.

All valance hems will need to be finished in some way. In particular, a shaped hem needs to be identified against the curtains when they are drawn. A bound edge is quite formal and fringe or fan edging braid is suitable for an informal room. The lining will show around the shaping, so make a facing with the front fabric, at least as deep as the shaping, or completely line the valance with the main fabric.

You will almost always need something to 'weigh' the lower edge down, but this need not be too much of a separate item. Stitching strips of a complementary color into the fabric before it is made up is a neat way to achieve this. You can

Opposite Shaping the lower edge of a valance softens the line and its center can be cut higher to allow in more light. Heavy bullion fringe stitched to the lower edge adds the weight needed for the valance to hang well.

either cut and join strips or set them like pin tucks.

Chunky woven edging looks good stitched to the bottom of a valance and to the sides and hems of heavy curtains, especially in an informal country situation. Ravishing combinations of colors and materials can be bought as cords, ropes, fan edgings and flat braids, any of which can transform an ordinary fabric into something quite distinctive.

Deep fringes add weight both visually and physically. Gathered valances, and especially those made of heavy fabric, will stick out if left plain, so force the hang with a thick fringe or chunky bullion. Always over scale, remembering that things look smaller when they are hanging above you. As a guide, a room two and half meters (eight feet) high, would need a valance of no less than 10 cm (4 in) and no more than 15 cm (6 in).

Never use fringes that are too short and almost never those with small bobbles, which should be kept for cushions and lampshades. Always check the color of the fringing in place. A lovely green and blue combination on the table could become sludge gray once it's hanging in front of the light. To preserve the color of a fringe and the weight of the valance, stitch the fringe onto the valance, so that the bottom of the fringe just lines up with the bottom of the fabric. Silk, cotton and linen fringes and braids, light in weight and in color, can be used to lighten the whole design and to add an extra, softer dimension. Stitched with the top of the fringe to the lower edge of the valance, so that the fringe hangs below, the light will filter through to soften the edges.

Distinctive styles

Frills are not as fashionable now as they were a few years ago, when they tended to be completely overdone in the most unsuitable situations. Frills should rarely be used in the drawing room, but do have a part to play in the most feminine bedrooms and boudoirs. Fabrics with a small rosebud print

Far left Gathered valances are chosen to soften a window: here the 'frilly' treatment makes a classic, contemporary bathroom a little more feminine.

Left Valances can be useful to cover an ugly space between the ceiling and the top of the window.

Right Before cutting a valance shape, make a paper template and pin in position. Then you can see how the curves relate to the window and to the style of the room. Hand-woven picot lace softens the edges and looks timeless with traditional blue and white toile de Jouy.

Right The soft pink binding echoes the mid-tones of the floral pattern. A gathered valance raises the visual height of the window and provides a convenient shelf for favorite bits and pieces.

used in small cottage windows can be quite sweet with frilled edges; and curtains in windows with recessed arms can benefit from frilled interest at the overlap.

For a masculine room — say, a study or book room — pleats are a good way in which to take up the fullness so that a soft valance can still be chosen. Design the size of pleat to relate to the size of the room and plan the fabric pattern so that any stripes or motifs are shown off to their best advantage. Allow approximately three times fullness and make up the valance as a long length, completely stitched. Fold the pleats and tack in place. Stitch a stiff curtain tape to the back of the valance, approximately one fifth of the overall depth from the top. Catch each pleat securely, using strong thread and back stitches. Stitch cord over the stitching line, making knots at the center of each pleat if you wish.

Simple, flat valance

◀◀ see also ▶▶
Curtain fittings p. 24
Attached valances p. 88

This valance is pleasing for its total simplicity: it frames the window and makes no other demands on the eye. Three different checks of the same color tone but differing scales all work together comfortably. The valance acts to border the curtain and to complete the effect of framing the window. It is a great idea if you've moved to a taller house and want to bring your existing curtains with you.

Making: Measure the width of the valance board and divide it into sections of anything between 20 and 40 cm (8 and 16 in). From a design point of view, the only strict rule is that each section is no more than the depth of the finished valance. Add 5 or 6 cm (2 or 2½ in) to each section to make the drape, and 5 cm (2 in) to each return. Make and cover the wooden valance board with fabric (see page 24).

Cut and join the lengths of fabric, interlining and lining. Even if the curtains are not interlined, use a fine domette for the soft drape. Lock the fabrics together, straighten the edges and bind the top and bottom edges with either a contrast color or the same fabric cut on the cross. This basic binding technique is illustrated on page 151. Cover one button for each section, plus two for the back of the returns.

Pin the valance to the board with upholstery tacks or large drawing pins. Stitch a button and tie at each section and to each end. If dust collects in the folds in time, just unpin and shake it out.

A printed linen chintz design and three different checks work harmoniously. When you are choosing several fabrics to use together, bear in mind that there should be only one dominant color, although several tones are pleasing. The backgrounds should be similar in weight and color and the scale of pattern should vary.

Gathered valance

◀◀ **see also** ▶▶
Curtain fittings p. 24
Herringbone stitch p. 146

Lock stitch p. 147
Gathering stitches p. 147

Gathered valances are charming in a cottage or farmhouse, where pretty prints, checks or stripes are in order. In an elegant, formal home, a soft valance is also suitable. Plain colored fabrics finished with fringes remain elegant for reception rooms and well designed floral chintzes come into their own in bedrooms.

Preparation: Take care to get the length right. The valance should fully cover all curtain and window fittings. Cut a paper template and pin it to the wall to make sure. No window frame or inside plasterwork should be visible and the top of the valance should either be right under the cornice or to the ceiling. There should be no thin shadow line between the top of the valance and the ceiling.

To make a valance board, follow the directions on page 24. Before assembling, cut the front to your own design. Paint it or cover it with fabric. Cut and join lengths of fabric, interlining and lining to approximately two and a half times fullness and the depth of the valance, plus hem allowances of 5–6 cm (2–2½ in). Join any border fabric you may want to the lower edge.

1 Lay the fabric onto the worktable, right side down. Press and pin it flat. Lay the interlining over, matching seams, and lock the two fabrics together at each seam. Pin the layers together along the top. Press the lower edge up by 6 cm (2½ in) along the hemline, then pin and herringbone all the way along.

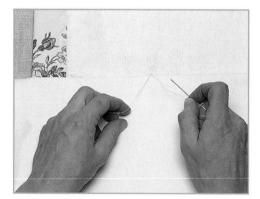

2 Lay the lining over, match seams and top edges. Lock the lining to the interlining at each seam and half way between.

3 Press the lining. Score along the hemline and trim along this line neatly. Press the lining hem 3 cm (1¼ in) under, pin and slip stitch to the valance fabric.

4 Check the overall drop. Run two gathering threads close to each other, approximately 2 cm (¾ in) from the raw edges. Pull up in sections of approximately 60 cm (24 in) and spread the gathers evenly in each.

5 Pin heading tape to the gathered edge, covering the gathering threads by just 0.5 cm (¼ in). Keep the gathers evenly spread. Machine stitch close to the edge of the heading tape and again 1.5 cm (⅝ in) higher. Fold the tape in half to enclose the raw edges and slip stitch from the back into the stitched line.

6 Secure to the inside of the valance board with large drawing pins or thumb tacks. Or use touch and close tape: machine stitch the soft side to the front of the heading tape before folding over. Staple the opposite side to the inside front of the wooden board.

Checks and chintzes have long been a favorite combination. Introducing the softer toile de Jouy under a scalloped valance serves to lighten this window treatment.

Basic Skills

All the ideas and projects in this book can be attempted if you master a few basic sewing skills in the first place. Depending upon your experience of making curtains, some or most of the skills outlined here may be familiar. Even so, it is useful to check that you are taking advantage of some of the tricks of the trade, or that you are doing things in the best or quickest way possible.

There are no real short cuts with basic sewing skills — you just have to learn them. But once you have them under your belt, the whole world of window treatments opens up, and you can allow your imagination and creativity full flow.

Seams

Pinning

When pinning two layers of fabric together or piping onto fabric, always use both horizontal and vertical pins to keep the fabric in place from both directions. The horizontal pins need to be removed just before the machine foot reaches them and the vertical ones — cross pins — can remain in place so that the fabrics are held together the whole time.

French seam

Use French seams for sheers and unlined curtains or on any occasion when a seam might be visible. Pin the fabrics together with the wrong sides facing. Stitch 0.5 cm (¼ in) from the raw edges. Trim and flip the fabric over, bringing the right sides together. Pin again, 1 cm (½ in) from the stitched edge and stitch along this line to enclose the raw edges. Press from the right side, always pressing the seam in one direction only.

Flat fell seam

This method neatens the seams of heavier weight fabrics. Pin the fabrics together with the right sides facing and stitch 1.5–3 cm (⅝–1 ¼ in) from the raw edges. Trim one seam to just under half. Fold the other over to enclose the raw edge. Press down. Stitch close to the fold line.

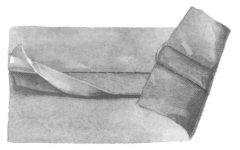

Flat seams

This is the most common and straightforward seam for normal use. With right sides together, pin 1.5–2 cm (⅝-¾ in) in from the edge at 10 cm (4 in) intervals. Pin cross pins halfway between each seam pin. These cross pins will remain in place while you are stitching to prevent the fabrics slipping. Once it is machine stitched, open the seam flat and press from the back. Press from the front. Now press from the back, under each flap, to remove the pressed ridgeline.

Below and below middle Flat seams are always used for joins where the fabric needs to lie flat – when joining stripes, blocks or patchwork to make the curtain front, for example.

Mitered corners

These are instructions for miters for the hems of any curtains. It is particularly important that the corners of interlined or heavy lined curtains are mitered as neatly as possible to reduce the bulk. You can trim the interlining away along the diagonal fold line before the miter is remade. The hems and sides for lined curtains are folded double, with the raw edges tucked inside. Allow approximately 12 cm (4¾ in) for the sides and either 12 cm (4¾ in) or 20 cm (8 in) for the hem. The hems and sides of interlined curtains are left raw to lie flat and are stitched over the raw edges.

When sides and hems are equal

Press the side seam over and the hem up. Position a pin through the point of the corner.

Open out the folds and turn in the corner at a 45 degree angle, with the pin at the center of the fold line.

Fold the hem up and the sides in again along the original fold lines. Keep the pin on the point and make sure the fabric is firmly tucked into the folded lines. If the hems and/or sides are to be folded double, you may want to cut the corner off to within 1.5 cm (⅝ in) of the fold to reduce the bulk.

When sides and hems are unequal

Press the side seam over and the hem up. Position a pin through the point of the corner. Angle away the fold of the corner towards the hem, leaving a longer fold on the side turnings so that the raw edges meet when the mitered corner is finished. You may have to fiddle a bit, but it is worth making sure that the sides and

hem do line up exactly when they are folded back. Depending on your allowances, it is worth starting with the point of the corner sitting on the folded hemline. Press lightly. Position pins at the corner and at the edge of the folds on hem and side.

Cut any interlining away, trimming along the fold line.

Fold side and hem back carefully, so that the two sides line up exactly.

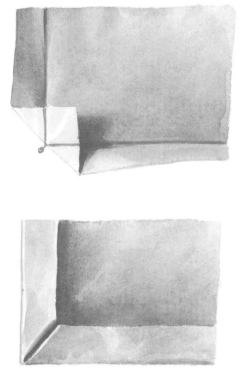

Stitches

Always ensure that you start and finish all stitching with a double stitch. Never use a knot, which is unreliable.

Hemming stitch

This stitch is used along the hems of lined curtains and the hems and sides of unlined curtains. Each stitch should be approximately 1.5 cm (⅝ in) in length. Slide the needle through the folded hem, pick up two threads of the main fabric and push the needle directly back into the fold.

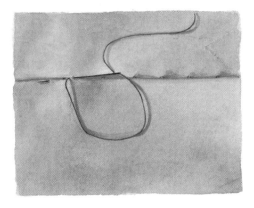

Herringbone stitch

Herringbone stitch is used over any raw edge that is then covered by another fabric. It is worked in the opposite direction to all other stitches, so right handers will work from left to right. Each whole stitch should be approximately 3 cm (1¼ in) for hems (a) and 8 cm (3¼ in) for

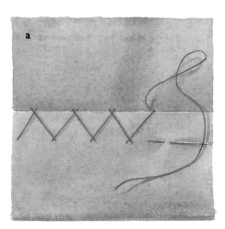

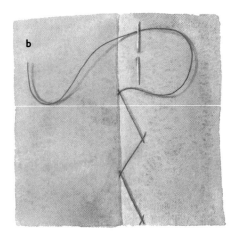

side turnings (b). Stitch into the hem, from right to left, and approximately 1.5 cm (⅝ in) to the right make a stitch into the curtain, picking up two threads. Pull through and stitch 1.5 cm (⅝ in) to the right, making a stitch into the hem.

Ladder stitch

Ladder stitch is used to join two folded edges invisibly together. Slide the needle along the fold 0.5 cm (¼ in) and straight into the fold opposite. Slide along for 0.5 cm (¼ in) and back into the first fold, again directly opposite.

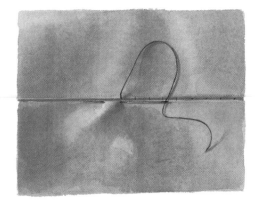

Long stitch

Long stitch is the most effective for the side turnings of interlined curtains, as it holds the interlining tight to the main fabric. Make a horizontal stitch approximately 1 cm (½ in) across. Bring the thread down diagonally by about 4 cm (1½ in) and repeat.

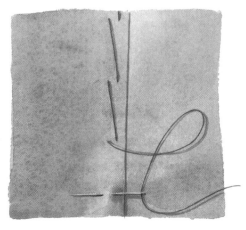

Slip stitch

This stitch is used to sew linings to curtains. Always use a color thread that matches the main fabric. Make each stitch approximately 1.5 cm (⅝ in). Slide the needle through the main fabric and pick up two threads of the lining. Push the needle back into the main fabric exactly opposite and slide through a further 1.5 cm (⅝ in).

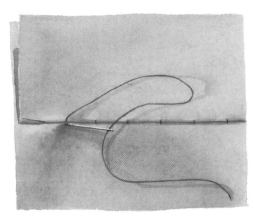

Lock stitch

This stitch holds linings, interlinings and fabrics together, preventing them from separating, but still allowing some degree of necessary movement. Always use thread that blends with the background of the curtain fabric and the lining color when stitching lining to interlining. Fold back the lining, secure the thread to the lining and make a small stitch in the main fabric just below. Make a large loop approximately 10 cm (4 in) long (slightly shorter for small items, such as valances) and make a small stitch in the lining inside this loop. Stitch into the main fabric. Do not pull the stitch too tightly, but allow it to remain slightly loose.

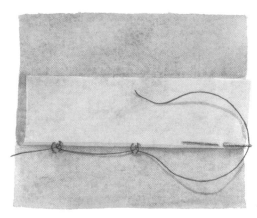

Gathering stitches

Run two threads almost together — that is, just a few millimeters apart, approximately 2 cm (¾ in) from the raw edge. If you are hand stitching, make sure the stitches are kept as level as possible so that the gathers pull up evenly.

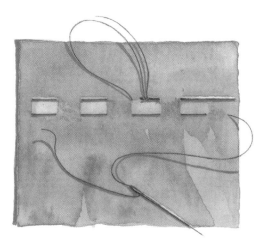

Buttonhole stitch

Of course, this stitch is used for buttonholes, but also wherever a raw edge needs to be strengthened or neatened. Work from left to right with the raw edge uppermost. Push the needle from the back to the front, approximately 0.3 cm (⅛ in) below the edge. Twist the thread around the needle and pull the needle through, carefully tightening the thread so that it knots right on the edge of the fabric to form a ridge.

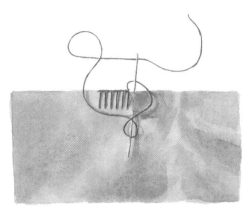

Blanket stitch

Originally used to neaten the raw edges of woollen blankets, this stitch is now mainly decorative. It is most comfortable worked from the side with the edge towards you. Push the needle from the front to the back, about 0.5 cm (¼ in) from the edge (this measurement will vary with large or small items). Hold the thread from the last stitch under the needle and pull up to make a loop on the edge.

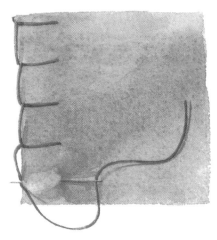

'Buttonholes' can be almost any size or shape and are not difficult to do — but it is perhaps best to practice on a scrap of fabric first.

Embroidery

We often use embroidery stitches to finish off curtains with a personal touch. If you are a keen embroiderer you can, of course, use any number of stitches to make the most interesting and complex edging designs. If you are less experienced, with memories only of a cross-stitched place mat embroidered at school, then you are probably best advised to stick to easy stitches to begin with. The idea to bear in mind is that the intent is to produce a design that is more interesting but not much more time consuming than hem stitch.

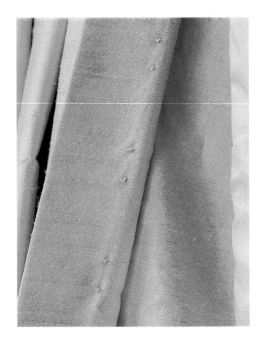

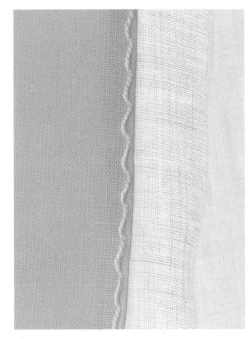

Make hems along the sides and hems of an unlined curtain, approximately 4 cm (1½ in) in depth. Stitch right through with French knots at regular intervals. Here the twin knots are about 1 cm (¼ in) apart with 5 cm (2 in) gaps between. To make a French knot, push the needle partly through to the front. Wind the thread three times around the needle, hold the spare thread lightly and pull the needle through, keeping the 'knot' shape. Don't let the knot go too tight or the needle will get stuck, or too loose that the knot is lost. Take the needle to the back, using this stitch to hold the knot in place. Run the thread through the folds to the next position.

Once a border has been stitched to the main fabric, make decorative herringbone stitches along the seamed edge. The stitches should be deep enough to accommodate — and so minimize — the seam inside. Use perle or embroidery threads and keep the stitches even.

Make a bordered curtain and then top stitch on the border side, close to the stitched edge. Thread a blunt needle with perle or embroidery thread and weave from left to right through every third machine stitch to make a very simple and quick pattern.

Make hems along the sides and hems of an unlined curtain, approx. 4 cm (1 ½ in) in depth. Stitch right through with single chain stitches at regular, but not rigid intervals. To make the stitch, push the needle partly through to the back and then up again about 0.5 cm (¼ in) away, with just a fraction of the point sticking though. Take the thread and make a loop around the point of the needle. Pull the needle through and then push back just the other side of the thread, securing the loop or 'chain'. Run the threads through the folds to the next position, so that they don't show. If both sides are visible, run back through the opposite side and make chains using the same sites.

Silk organdy curtains are ethereal in appearance, and were chosen here to confine a mezzanine area by suggestion, rather than covering it entirely. This is not a project for a complete amateur, but an experienced needlewoman would be able to follow the stitches with a little practice. Find a good, illustrated, embroidery stitch handbook. Several complex stitches have been used here, both to lace the organdy and to make attractive hems. But even if you can only do stem and chain stitches, you can still create plenty of interesting designs. Feather stitch was used to join the hem sections to the main body, but ladder stitch or drawn threadwork could be selected for similar effect.

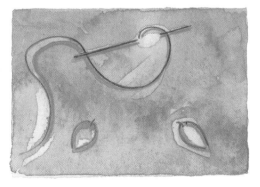

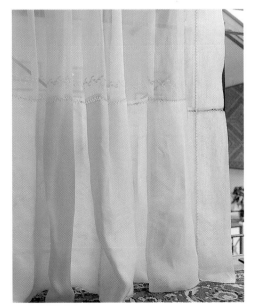

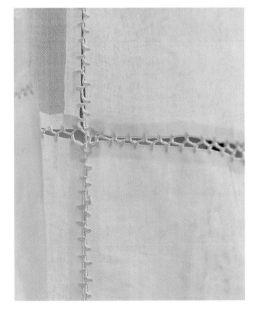

Bought trimmings

All trimmings should be pinned on completely before they are stitched. Don't stretch the trimmings as you pin and stitch, as the fabric will wrinkle, and if you let the trimming hang too loose, it will bow and buckle.

Fringing

Place the trimming so that only the fringe itself extends beyond the edge of the fabric. Slip stitch just the top edge if the fringe is designed to be hanging down. If the fringe is to hang on the leading edge of a curtain, then the bottom of the flat tape should be stitched to the very edge of the curtain. Stitch it on from the curtain front side.

Fan edge braid

Place so that only the bottom fan extends beyond the fabric. Catch a single loop in place at the inner edge of each fan, unless the fan shapes are oversized, in which case the center of the fan will also need to be attached. Also catch the inner edge of the lower fan to the edge of the curtain.

Flat braid

Slip stitching can show up along the edges of flat braid. There will usually be a ridge — however small — on each side. Neat, tiny running stitches just inside the ridge will be the least obvious way to attach any flat braid.

Cord or rope

Be careful not to over twist or unwind the cord as you are pinning it on. In the worst case, the edges of the curtains will kink and bow; and if the cord is made with more than one color, the individual strands of the twists will show up. Pick up the same color each time at the same regular intervals. Aim for 1 cm (½ in) for 0.6 cm (¼ in) cord to 2 cm (¾ in) for 1.2 cm (½ in) cord.

Below Cords, fringes, tassels and edgings — shown here in five different window treatments — should always echo the fabric colors in order to add depth and interest.

Borders and bindings

Making

For a 1.5 cm (⅝ in) border for one edge with 6 cm (2½ in) behind, cut strips 9 cm (3½ in) wide. Join lengths if necessary, always on the cross, to make the required length. Pin the strip to the fabric, right sides together and stitch 1.4 cm (slightly less than ⅝ in) from the raw edges. For an unlined curtain, once the binding has been pressed to the back, fold under in half so that the binding shows 1.5 cm (⅝ in) from the front and the back.

Bordering a corner

Stop pinning short of the corner by the width of the finished border. Fold the strip back on itself to make a sharp angle and pin across this fold line. Pin on the adjacent side, the same distance from the edge. Stitch, stopping at the pin and secure. Begin stitching again at the same point on the adjacent side. Press to miter. Fold fabric to the back, mitering in the opposite direction. Miter the corner carefully, especially if a strip or check fabric is being used.

Bordered headings

For gathered headings, cut the strips to double the width of the finished border, plus enough to go to the bottom of the gathers. For a 2 cm (¾ in) border and a heading frill of 9 cm (3½ in), cut 14 cm (5½ in) strips.

In order to make flat headings, cut three times the width of the finished border, plus 2 cm (¾ in).

For pleated headings, cut twice the width of the finished border, plus the depth of the heading, plus 5 cm (2 in).

Trim the raw edges to 1.4 cm (slightly less than ⅝ in). Press from the front, pressing away from the main fabric. Fold the border strip to the back, measuring the edge to 1.5 cm (⅝ in). Keep the fabric tucked firmly into the fold and pin at 8 cm (3¼ in) intervals. Turn to the back and herringbone the raw edge to the main fabric.

Above right Binding the edges of unlined curtains is a good way to deal with the raw edges.

Right Binding on light muslin adds enough weight for the sheer curtains to hang well.

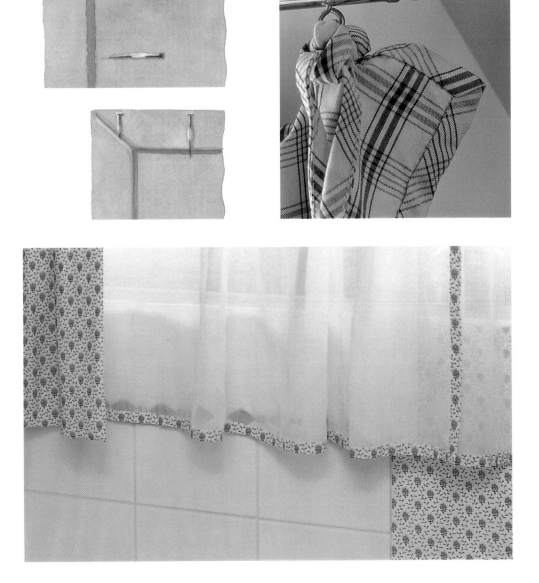

Ties

Ties are both practical and decorative and are used extensively throughout soft furnishings. For example, ties are used for securing cushion sides and seat pads and for fastening loose covers. For curtains, they are used primarily to tie a heading to a ring or pole. The length and width of the ties depends on the window treatment design. Ties chosen purely as a means to hold curtain to pole will be less significant and smaller than those chosen for decorative effect. Ties that just knot into a ring need to be a minimum of 20 cm (8 in) and can be up to 40 cm (16 in) long. If you want to make a bow, 40 cm (16 in) is probably the minimum possible length.

Don't forget to take the diameter of the pole into consideration, and ties that thread through small rings should be no more than 1.5 cm (⅝ in) wide. If you can put the fittings up before the curtains themselves are finished, pin strips of spare fabric or tape to the top to check the best length and width. You will need two ties for each position.

Simple tiebacks can be made using long ties, such as those made for the luxurious silk curtains on page 83. The simple cotton gingham curtains on page 68 show how effective oversized ties can be to hold back curtains.

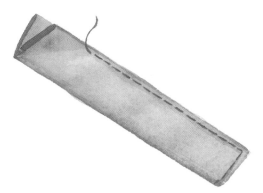

Folded ties

To make folded ties, cut a strip of fabric four times the proposed width of the finished tie and 3 cm (1¼ in) longer. Press one short end under by 1 cm (½ in). Press the tie in half lengthwise, fold each side into the middle, press it again and then fold and stitch it together close to the folded edges.

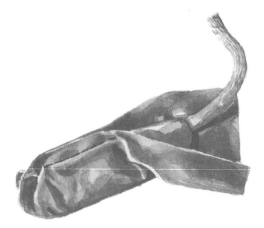

Rouleau ties

To make rounded, rouleau ties cut a strip of fabric four times the width of the finished tie and 3 cm (1¼ in) longer. Fold in half lengthwise, right sides together, enclosing a piece of cord that is longer than the strip of fabric. Stitch along the short side to secure the cord firmly. If the rouleau is quite wide, knot the cord. Stitch along the length, 0.2 cm (⅛ in) towards the raw edge from the center.

Trim the fabric across the corner, pull the cord through, at the same time turning the fabric right side out. Cut off the cord at the end. Press the raw edge under and slip stitch with small stitches.

Sashes

Sashes are really just oversized ties. For a room of average size, allow two pieces of fabric 1.5 meters (5 feet) in length and 30–50 cm (12–20 in) wide. Fold the fabric in half lengthwise, right sides together, then taper the ends and pin these and the long sides together. Stitch 1.5 cm (⅝ in) from the raw edges. Turn right side out. Fold under the raw edges and stitch together. Fold into a fan shape approximately 3–4 cm (1¼–1½ in) from the end and stitch securely. Stitch a tieback ring to the back.

Ties are decorative as well as functional. They can be fixed close to the fitting to hang down decoratively, or be used to their full length.

Piping

If piping is to be used in straight lines, it is easiest to cut it straight. If it is to be bent around corners, then it should be cut on the cross. For 4 mm (⅛ in) piping cord, cut 4 cm (1½ in) wide strips. All joins should be made on the cross to minimize bulk when the fabric is folded.

To cut on the straight

Cut lengths as long as possible. Hold two strips, butting the ends together as if making a continuous length. Trim away both corners at a 45-degree angle. Hold together and flip the top one over. Stitch where the two pieces cross.

To cut on the cross

With the fabric flat on the table, fold one bottom corner as if making a 30 cm (12 in) square. Cut along the fold line. Mark pencil lines from this cut edge at 4 cm (1½ in) intervals and cut along these lines. Hold two pieces, butting the ends together as if making a continuous strip. Flip the top one over and stitch together where the two fabrics cross.

Making up and pinning on

Press seams flat and cut away excess corners. Fold in half along the length and insert the piping cord. Always pin piping so that the raw edges of the piping line up with those of the main fabric. Machine stitch to encase approximately 0.2 cm (⅛ in) from the cord. Keep the fabric folded exactly in half.

To bend piping around curves, snip into the stitching line for the piping to lie flat. For a right angle, stop pinning 1.5 cm (⅝ in) from the corner, snip the piping right to the stitching line, fold the piping to 90 degrees and start pinning 1.5 cm (⅝ in) on the adjacent side.

Joining

To join piping, overlap by approximately 6 cm (2½ in). Unpick the casing on one side and cut away the cord so that the two ends butt up. Fold the piping fabric across at a 45-degree angle and cut along this fold. Fold under 1 cm (½ in). Fold this over the cased piping and pin together as tightly as possible. Pin to the fabric and stitch close to the piping. For a very thick fabric, thin the cord itself back a little as well.

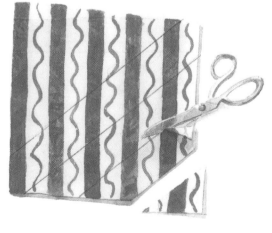

Piping the border to the curtain adds a tailored detail in keeping with the formality of the curtain.

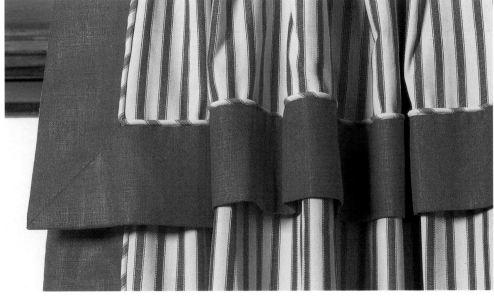

Glossary

FIBERS

Acrylic: Man-made from petroleum, often mixed with more expensive fibers to keep the cost down. Not hard-wearing, but useful for permanent pleating.

Cotton: A natural fiber, it is very versatile, woven, knitted and mixed with other fibers. Use for any soft furnishings according to weight. It will lose strength in direct sunlight, so protect. Soft, strong, easy to launder, washable if preshrunk.

Linen: Fibers found inside the stalks of the flax plant are woven to make linen cloth in almost any weight. Distinctive slub weave, from very fine linen for under curtains and sheers to heavy upholstery weight. A very strong fiber which is easy to work and will take high temperatures.

Silk: From the cocoon of the silk worm, silk is soft and luxurious to touch. Fades in sunlight, so protect. Available in every weight, suitable for soft furnishings, from lamp shades to heavy upholstery. Good mixed with cotton or wool.

Wool: A natural fiber, liable to excessive shrinkage as the 'scales' on each fiber overlap, harden and 'felt'. Is warm to touch and initially resists damp. Ideal for upholstery and curtains.

Viscose: Wood pulp woven into fibers which mixes well with other fibers helping them to take dyes and fireproofing. Washable and sheds dirt easily.

FABRICS

Brocade: Traditionally woven fabric using silk, cotton, wool or mixed fibers, on a jacquard loom, in a multi- or self-colored floral design. Brocades drape well and can be used for curtains, traditional bed drapes, covers and upholstery. Some are washable but most will need dry cleaning.

Calico: Coarse, plain weave cotton in cream or white with 'natural' flecks in it. Available in many widths and weights for inexpensive curtains, bed drapes, garden awnings. Wash before use to shrink and press while damp.

Cambric: Closely woven, plain weave fabric from linen or cotton with a sheen on one side. Use, wash and press as calico. Widely used for cushion pad covers but also for curtains.

Canvas: Plain weave cottons in various weights suitable for upholstered chair covers, inexpensive curtains, slip covers, awnings and outdoor use. Available as unbleached, coarse cotton or more finely woven and dyed in strong colors.

Chintz: Cotton fabric with 'Eastern' design using flowers and birds, often with a resin finish which gives a characteristic sheen or glaze and which also repels dirt. The glaze will eventually wash out, so only dry clean curtains. Avoid using steam to press and never fold as the glaze will crack.

Corduroy: A strong fabric woven to form vertical ribs by floating extra yarn across, which is then cut to make the pile. Use for traditional upholstery. Press on a velvet pin board while damp.

Crewel: Plain or hop sack woven, natural cotton background embroidered in chain stitch in cream or multi-colored wools. Soft but heavy, lovely for curtains, soft shades, cushions and light-use loose covers. May be washed but test a small piece first.

Damask: A jacquard fabric first woven in Damascus with satin floats on a warp satin background in cotton, silk, wool and mixed fibers in various weights. Use for curtains, drapes and sometimes covers and upholstery, choosing different weights for different uses. Make up reversed if a matte finish is required. Suitable for curtaining which will be seen from both sides.

Gingham: Plain weave fabric in 100% cotton with equal width strips of white plus one other color in both warp and weft threads to produce blocks of checks or stripes. Use for small windows in 'cottagey' rooms, kitchens, children's bedrooms and slip covers. Mix with floral patterns and other checks and stripes.

Holland: Firm, hard-wearing fabric made from cotton or linen stiffened with oil or shellac. Use for shades, lightweight covers, curtaining and valances.

Lace: Open-work fabrics in designs ranging from simple spots to elaborate panels. Usually in cotton or a cotton and polyester mixture.

Moiré: A finish usually on silk or acetate described as 'watermarked'. The characteristic moiré markings are produced by pressing plain woven fabric through hot engraved cylinders which crush the threads and push them into different directions to form the pattern. This finish will disappear on contact with water, so it is not suitable for upholstery.

Muslin: White or off-white, inexpensive, open-weave cloth which can be dyed in pastel colors. Use for under-curtains and sheers in hot countries to filter light and insects.

Organdy: The very finest cotton fabric with an acid finish giving it a unique crispness. Use for lightweight curtains, dressing tables and lamp shades. Wash and press while damp.

Organza: Similar to organdy and made of silk, polyester or viscose. Very springy and used for stiffening headings of fine fabrics, shades to filter sunlight and to protect curtains. Use layers of varying tones together.

Provençal prints: Small printed designs onto fine cotton for curtains, upholstery, cushions and covers. Washable, hard-wearing, the best hardly crease. Originally Indian designs, now mostly printed in Provence.

Silk voile: Light to medium weight silk, relatively inexpensive for curtaining. Not a great range of colors, but the natural slub and matte finish are attractive.

Silk shantung: Light silk woven with irregular yarns giving a dull sheen. Use to line bed curtains, as under curtains where protected from sunlight, and lamp shades. Shantung gathers and frills easily and drapes well. Use lots of fullness. Available in a huge range of colors.

Taffeta: The best is 100% silk but can be woven from acetate and blends. The acetates are most useful where the look of silk is wanted without the danger of rotting or fading in direct sunlight.

Tartan: Authentic plaids belong to individual Scottish clans and are woven in fine wool twill, originally for kilts. Available in several weights – use the heaviest for upholstery and heavy curtains and the finest for light curtains. The fabric is the same on both sides, so use for doorways and unlined curtains.

Ticking: Traditional cotton herringbone weave in black and white used for mattresses and pillow covers. Very dense weave, and good for inexpensive stylish curtains.

Toile de Jouy: Pastoral designs in tones of a single color on a calico ground. Sometimes now on colored grounds; the best designs are engraved copper plate and hand-printed. For curtains, upholstery, lamp shades, cushions.

Tweed: Wool worsted cloth in hound's tooth check and muted stripes and checks. Mainly from Scotland and Ireland, the suiting quality is hard-wearing yet drapes very well. Good for upholstery and curtains especially for country use.

Velvet: Available in cotton, wool, linen and silk. The fine pile throws the light and the cloth looks a much lighter color upside down. Careful stitching is needed so that the fabrics don't 'walk' on each other as the opposite piles meet. Pull a small piece of the cloth to test the quality. If it pulls out easily the cloth won't stand even one cleaning without weakening.

Voile: Fine lightweight cotton or linen or wool. Any color available. Use for fine curtains, bed curtains and drapes. Choose one which will wash and dry easily. Good polyester voile looks just like cotton, is usually fireproof and will wash and dry like a dream.

AUTHOR'S ACKNOWLEDGMENTS

Many thanks to those suppliers who have helped us with some wonderful fabrics for this project: Osborne and Little (020 8675 2255); Northcroft Fabrics (01628 488700) and Busby and Busby (01258 881211).

There have been many hands at work to produce this book, who deserve both recognition and thanks. Without those friends and clients who not only commissioned me to design their rooms but then also most generously allowed us to photograph the results, this book would not have been possible. Only the expertise of talented seamstresses Sarah Westcott, Jackie Pullman and Julie Toop could have made the windows look as good as they do. Thanks also to the New Holland publishing team: Rosemary, Coral, Yvonne and Kate; to Peter Crump for his clear design and to Judy Spours for organizing and editing. Special thanks to John Freeman for constant support and wonderful pictures; to Carol for the use of her hands in the photographs; to Michael and Rowan for their hard work in preparation and styling and to Yvonne, Don, Peter and Lisa.

PICTURE CREDITS

p.6 (bottom left) David Johnson, p.13 Zimmer & Rohde, p.37 (top right and bottom right) David Johnson, p.46 (top) Pierre Frey, p.53 (bottom) David Johnson, p.54 Heather Luke, p.55 David Johnson, p.62 (top left) Heather Luke, p.65 (right) Timney Fowler, p.82 (bottom) David Johnson, p.87 (bottom) Heather Luke, p.101 (top) David Johnson, p.101 Heather Luke, p.122 (bottom) David Johnson, p.123 (top left) Heather Luke, p.123 (bottom left) Heather Luke, p.137 (top) David Johnson, p.137 (bottom)

Suppliers

USA

Most large department stores carry a good range of fabrics, fittings, and accessories. Look in the Yellow Pages for details of your nearest fabric store or drapery retailer.

Trenton Haberdashery
1816 Pennington Rd.
Trenton, NJ 08618
(609) 882-0703

A to Z Window Treatment Corporation
64 W. 48th St.
New York, NY 10036
(212) 869-5990

Class Window Treatment
1459 1st Ave
New York, NY 10011
(212) 472-8600

Paris Drapery
2846 N. Milwaukee Ave
Chicago, IL 60618
(773) 486-7330

Vogue Fabric Store
718 Main St.
Evanston, IL 60202
(847) 864-9600
www.myvoguefabrics.com

Hancock Fabrics
4848 W. Irving Park Rd.
Chicago, IL 60641
(773) 286-8550

Best Fabrics
10901 Harry Hines Blvd.
Dallas, TX
(214) 350-2583

Dallas Drapery Shop
2970 Blystone Ln, #109
Dallas, TX 75220
(214) 654-0177

Pierre Deux French Country
134 Maiden Lane
San Francisco, CA 94108
(415) 296-9940

Dreams Fabric &
Custom Sewing
921 Howard St.
San Francisco, CA 94103
(415) 543-1800

Excellent Fabrics
420 Grant Ave
San Francisco, CA 94108
(415) 421-7795

Exquisite Fabrics Inc
1775 K St. NW
Washington, DC 20006
(202) 775-1818

MPM Fabrics
1317 E. Capitol St. SE
Washington, DC 20003
(202) 234-4778

Couture Fabrics of Alexandria
1703 Belle View Blvd., #B1
Alexandria, VA 22307
(703) 768-8500

Jo Ann Fabrics & Crafts
5900 N. Port Washington Rd.
Milwaukee, WI 53217
(414) 332-5533

Hancock Fabrics Inc.
3555 S. 27th St., #7
Milwaukee, WI 53221
(414) 384-3990

Pacific Fabric and Crafts
2230 4th Ave. S.
Seattle, WA 98134
(206) 628-6237
www.pacificfabrics.com

Seattle Fabrics
8702 Aurora Ave N.
Seattle, WA 98103
(206) 525-0670

Plenty of Textiles
2909 NE Blakeley St.
Seattle, WA 98105
(206) 524-4383

Pierre Deux
3500 Peachtree Rd. NE, #E10
Atlanta, GA 30326
(404) 869-7790

Atlanta Architectural Textiles
737 Miami Cir NE
Atlanta, GA 30324
(404) 231-9318

CANADA

Designer Fabric Outlet
1360 Queen St. W.
Toronto, ON M6K IL7
(416) 531-2810

Bobrowski Textiles
1306 St. Clair Ave. W.
Toronto, ON M6E ICI
(416) 654-8012

Drapes & Sew Much More
231 Carlton St.
Toronto, ON M5A 2L2
(416) 964-3778

Fabricland
5357 103 St. NW
Edmonton, AB T6H 4P8
(780) 438-5119

Fanny's Fabrics
6835 83 St. NW
Edmonton, AB T6C 2X9
(780) 465-9789

House of Fabrics
Metrotown Shopping Center
Vancouver, BC
(604) 436-9430

Index